THE
ATONEMENT
of JESUS
CHRIST

DR. EMMANUEL ABU KISSI

THE ATONEMENT OF JESUS CHRIST

iUniverse books may be ordered through booksellers or by contacting:

iUniverse
1663 Liberty Drive
Bloomington, IN 47403
www.iuniverse.com
1-800-Authors (1-800-288-4677)

ISBN: 978-1-5320-9034-9 (sc)
ISBN: 978-1-5320-9036-3 (hc)
ISBN: 978-1-5320-9035-6 (e)

Library of Congress Control Number: 2020901290

Print information available on the last page.

iUniverse rev. date: 04/06/2020

CONTENTS

CHAPTER 1

WHAT IS MAN?

The psalmist poses a question that is pertinent to our discussion of the fall of man. He says in Psalm 8:3–4 "When I consider thy heavens, the work of thy fingers, the moon and the stars, which thou has ordained, what is man, which thou art mindful of him? And the son of man, that thou visitest him."

God's concern about man surprised the psalmist. To the psalmist, man is insignificant amongst God's creation. It is helpful to examine what God taught Abraham about man. Man was a spirit—or, in other words, intelligence. How did man, being a spirit, become a living soul?

ABRAHAM

Abraham was an ordinary man who had the privilege of walking with God. Abraham was the great grandson of Noah through the lineage of Shem. The children of Noah were Japheth, Shem, and Ham, in that order. If I were to speculate on the reasons for the change of the order of lineage that names Shem first, I should make comparison with Jacob and his sons. For a good reason, Jacob cursed his firstborn, Reuben, instead

1

and promoted Juda to be the leader of his sons. He also gave the right of the firstborn to Joseph, who was the firstborn of Racheal, whom he married as his first wife. That was the day recorded in the scriptures as the wedding day for Jacob and Racheal. No reason has been given as to why Japheth also lost the right of the firstborn, as did Reuben. In any case, there is a reason why Abraham, being in the lineage of the second born, Shem, was given the right of the firstborn.

Abraham and his fathers lived in the city of Ur in the land of Chaldea. According to Abraham, his fathers, descendants of Shem, became idolatrous. Because Abraham continued to live the law of God, his father saw him as rebellious. Thus, Abraham's father decided to sacrifice him to the gods of Elkenah and of Egypt. In Abraham 1:9 we read that God sent an angel to deliver Abraham from the attempted assassination.

Abraham narrates the beginning of his relationship with God and writes that God said, "Behold, I will lead thee by my hand, and I will take thee, to put upon thee my name, even the priesthood of thy fathers, and my power shall be over thee" (Abraham 1:18). God asked Abraham to leave Ur, his kindred, and his father's house. He first moved to Harran, where he spent some years. Abraham then journeyed down south and settled in Damascus, before travelling to Egypt.

Before Abraham left for Egypt, God taught him about the sun, the moon, and the stars. The Lord revealed to Abraham the eternal nature of spirits. Abraham learned about pre-Earth life, foreordination, the creation, the choosing of a redeemer, and the second estate of man. God told Abraham, "…I show these things unto thee before ye go into Egypt that ye may declare all these words."

God, in his walk with Abraham, taught him many things. Living forever in immortality was not a question when man lived as a spirit in heaven. Neither was being unable to continue to live forever in immortality. Men had neither body nor the breath of life. It was impossible then to deprive the spirit of body or breath of life, as happens when a person dies. The spirit neither lives nor dies. Notwithstanding that some spirits are more intelligent than others, they have no beginning, they existed before, they shall have no end, and they shall exist after, for they are "gnolaum", or eternal. The Lord finally concludes, "I am the Lord thy God, I am more intelligent than they all. I dwell in the midst of them all; I now, therefore, have come down unto thee to declare unto thee the works which my hands have made, wherein my wisdom excelleth them all for I rule in the heavens above and in the earth beneath in all wisdom and prudence, over all the intelligences thine eyes have seen from the beginning; I came down in the beginning in the midst of all the intelligences thou hast seen" (Abraham 3:19, 21).

The teaching given to Abraham about the nature of spirits is interesting knowledge. This subject was almost put to rest until the prophet Joseph Smith also talked about the spirits. Abraham was born 1996 BC and Joseph Smith was born in AD 1805. The difference in time between the births of Abraham and Joseph Smith is 3,801 years. Adam, Enoch, Noah, Melchizedek, Abraham, Moses, and the dispensation of Jesus Christ have since passed. The last dispensation of time is that of Joseph Smith. In other words, it is the dispensation of the fullness of time.

The prophet Joseph Smith had several communications with the heavens. As a result, he has contributed as a messenger of God to the discussion on the nature of spirits. On May 6, 1833, the prophet Joseph Smith received the revelation of the Doctrine and Covenants 93. That message teaches that for a long time before He created the earth, man, being a spirit, was with God. But though eternal, he could not have the fullness of joy.

Now God desired all to become like him. He designed a plan that allowed the spirit man to be immortal and have eternal life and the fullness of joy. The Lord answered Moses and said that He had many heavens, and that the earths and their heavens would pass away to be replaced by others. He declared also, "For behold, this is my work and my glory to bring to pass the immortality and eternal life of man" (Moses 1:39). Several centuries earlier, the Lord had said to Abraham, "(there is nothing that the Lord thy God shall take in his heart to do but what he will do it)" (Abraham 3:17).

At the time in the beginning, God planned the existence of man to be in three estates. The first estate was when man was only an intelligence or spirit and did not have the fullness of joy. He was just to exist eternally as a spirit being in the spirit world. The second estate was on the earth, where man would need a body to live and experience the fullness of joy. Having a body of flesh and bones was a prerequisite to live on the earth. Having the fullness of joy was quite enviable. God said, "We will prove them herewith if they will do all things whatsoever the Lord their God will command them" (Abraham 3:25).

The foregoing chapter one teaches us that man existed as spirit before he was transformed into the living human being. In heaven, as a spirit, man had certain limitations. There were different levels of intelligence, and of course, some were more intelligent than others.

God wanted man to be like him, so He created a body with elements of the earth as a tabernacle, or a dwelling, for man, who was only a spirit. Man needed the body to be able to live on the earth. The spirits in heaven do not have bodies as human beings do. They do not have the breath of life either.

As God wanted his spirit children in heaven to be like him and be able to live on the earth, it is only reasonable to infer that God also has a body of flesh and bones, for he made man in his likeness and image. That means that in his image, man looks like God. Also, regarding his behaviour, one could say "Like Father, like son." In other words, God becomes happy and angry, and even weeps when He is sad. Just as parents on earth worry about the welfare and safety of their children, so also does God, our father in heaven, worry about us.

CHAPTER 2

THE PLAN OF REDEMPTION

PROBATION

Being a parent, our heavenly Father, a just and merciful God, pronounced a death sentence on Adam and Eve. Thereafter he set out to reorganize Adam's way forward. Recognizing his dual position as a just and merciful God, the Book of Mormon prophet Nephi marvelled at God's plan. He marvelled most at our probationary state. He says in 2 Nephi 9:10, "O how great the goodness of our God who prepareth a way for our escape from the grasp of this awful monster, yea, that monster, death and hell, which I call the death of the body, and also the death of the spirit" (In which the spirit is ostracized, never to be with the eternal God).

A time was granted unto man in which he might repent. Adam was immortal before the fall. With the fall, he would immediately have been ostracized. From the account on the fall in the garden of Eden, it appears that at the time of the fall, Adam and Eve had no children. The death penalty had been deferred as a suspended judgement. The man had been modified, however. The spirit, body, and breath of life continued as a living soul, but immortality had been withheld in this corruptible state of the suspended death sentence. It is in this state of the suspended death sentence, in mortality, that Adam had his children. This has continued until now.

During the probationary period of the suspended death sentence, as mentioned in Psalm 90:10 and Genesis 6:3, life was limited to 70 to 80 years, and also to 120 years. In ancient times, though, some died at a much older age. Additionally, a second law was given during this period of probation.

> Therefore, God gave unto them commandments, after having made known unto them the plan of redemption, that they should not do evil, the penalty thereof being a second death, which was an everlasting death as to things pertaining unto righteousness, for on such the plan of redemption could have no power, for the works of justice could not be destroyed according to the goodness of God. But God called upon men, in the name of his son (this being the plan of redemption which was laid) saying: If ye will repent, and harden not your hearts, then shall I have mercy upon you, through mine Only Begotten Son. Therefore, whosoever repenteth, and hardeneth not his heart, he shall have claim on mercy through my Only Begotten Son, unto a remission of his sins, and these shall enter into my rest. (Alma 12:32–34)

This means that man is on probation, which is a corrective measure. It is really a prison where man is expected to change his ways to become fit and to qualify again to live with God. If man does well, it will benefit him. Otherwise, God will be provoked and he will have another punishment following this period of probation.

With this knowledge, man must advice himself to avoid a second punishment, which will be permanent. God has a comfortable plan for us to go back home to live with Him, and so we must be very careful this time and become qualified to enter into the kingdom of God. Man has been given a second chance.

At the end of this period of probation, man dies. Justice implements full judgement and invokes the suspended death. The breath of life leaves, the body is dumped, and the spirit man departs. The bodies of both the righteous and the wicked remain in the grave, or death. The spirits of the wicked become captives and are imprisoned in hell. The spirits of the righteous, however, are received into the paradise of God.

The atonement, however, effects the resurrection of the dead, and man comes back to life the second time never to die again. Man, however, goes for judgement to determine his dwelling place in heaven for all eternity. Judgement takes cognizance of the thoughts, words, and actions of each individual during the probationary period of life in mortality. The judgement thus differentiates between the disobedient and the penitent to assign heavenly abodes accordingly. (See Revelation 20:12–13 in the Bible).

THE LAW OF PROBATION: JUSTICE AND MERCY

God himself is the originator of the law. Where there is no law, there is no punishment. Without the law, there would be no sin, and of necessity, there is punishment affixed to the law. The apostle Paul teaches this subject in his epistle to the Romans and says in Romans 7:8, "For without the law sin is dead."

Justice claims the disobedient and inflicts punishment, which is a state of misery. Mercy, however, claims the obedient and the penitent to effect redemption, but the plan of mercy cannot ignore justice and the punishment affixed to the law.

What happens if an indispensable person infringes the law? In such a situation, a reconciliatory plan might make a legally acceptable adjustment to rectify the situation. This is illustrated in the book of Leviticus 27:31–32. The law of Moses allowed a choice ram to be redeemed by payment of an additional 20 per cent of the estimated cost. The reconciliatory measure allows the one redeeming to voluntarily offer more than what he receives. The redeemer gives away a lot more. How is this tithing function with the ram referred to in the book of Leviticus (the law of Moses) linked to the atonement of Jesus Christ? After the fall, God gave commandments to Adam and Eve, as we read in Moses 5:5–8. Briefly, Adam was taught that blood sacrifice was a similitude of the sacrifice of the Only Begotten of the Father, which is full of grace and truth. Rams were thus almost synonymous with the Lamb of God (as John the Baptist referred to Jesus Christ).

During the practice of Judaism under the law of Moses, lambs were sacrificed at the temple. Such sacrifices were in the similitude of the sacrifice of the Only Begotten of the Father, the Lamb of God. These lambs were used as propitiation to reconcile the Israelites and the law of Moses. The Israelites knew that the millions of sacrificial animals symbolized Jesus Christ, the Messiah who was to come. But did they recognize him when he was with them?

The law requiring sacrifices was fulfilled when the blood of the Lord poured out of him unto the earth. And thus, in Christ the law of Moses is fulfilled, as recorded in Alma 34:13 and 3 Nephi 9:17, 19. If Adam's mission had failed, the desire of God to populate the earth would have been thwarted. To prevent any failure, God himself atoned for the sins of the world. His plan of mercy appeased the demands of justice that God might be a perfect, just, and merciful God.

Laws are made with punishment attached, but mercy grants repentance. Otherwise, justice takes its course to implement the full rigours of the law. The atonement brings mercy to effect the resurrection of the dead to bring back men, restoring man into the presence of God. Men are then judged not as disembodied spirits but as fully resurrected living souls who will never die again. The man is thereafter in immortality and eternal life.

Mercy cannot annul justice; that should not happen. This will certainly not be allowed in the courts of God. Thus, from the foundation of the world, God has established his own legal system. This brings salvation and redemption to man. God planned a system to circumvent Adam's immediate death by instituting an atonement to satisfy justice and mercy together. This would require an innocent third person to stand between the justice of the law and the mercy which will be made available at the expense of the intermediary. The atonement is to reconcile two estranged parties: justice of the law, and mercy.

The holy Messiah came to the rescue because he is full of grace and truth. He actually offers himself as a sacrifice for sin to answer the ends of the law for only those who have a broken heart and contrite spirit. The prophet Alma discusses this and asks if one could imagine how very important it is to make these things known to all people, that they may know that there is no flesh that can dwell in the presence of God except through the merits, mercy, and grace of the holy Messiah, for he lays down his life and takes it again by the power of the spirit that he may bring to pass the resurrection of the dead, being the first that should rise.

As it is now, he is the firstborn of God, inasmuch as he will make intercession for all the children of men, and they that believe in him shall be saved. Therefore, the demands of the law which the Holy One has given is the punishment thereof. This punishment is as mighty as the happiness which is the blessing to answer the suffering of the atonement.

Thus, the answering of the ends of the law means that the punishment affixed to the infringement of the law has been fulfilled. In the same vein, answering the ends of the atonement requires that an adequate blessing is given. This blessing compensates for the suffering during the performance of the atonement. The atonement, or propitiation, is a sacrifice to reconcile estranged parties. Justice of the law is one party. It demands adequate punishment for the offence committed against the law. Merciful kindness is the other party, and it brings man to immortality and eternal life.

CHAPTER 3

DEATH, RESURRECTION AND ATONEMENT

Adam's disobedience in the garden of Eden brought to him death, which passed upon all men. That death sentence had to be reversed. The power to bring man back from death was needed for God's plan of immortality and eternal life to be fulfilled. By Adam's sin all men were destined to die. For God's plan to be successful, there was need for power of resurrection to keep Adam alive. Actually, all men were in the same boat with Adam, and the power of the resurrection was to benefit all mankind.

The prophets in those days were concerned that a benefit of the atonement would be short-lived if the atonement was not infinite. In that case, the bodies would be disintegrated permanently, and there would be no resurrection. And if that should happen, then their spirits would remain permanently subject to the devil, who would then be their master permanently. That would mean that all spirits from heaven would finally end up being devils, because they would be agents to the devil. All would then be shut out from the presence of God, and all would become devils. This means that all would be stirred up unto secret combinations of murder and all manner of secret works of darkness. Fortunately, because of his great goodness, God has prepared a way for man to escape from the grasp of the monstrous devil.

These ancient prophets described two deaths for one person. They consider death of the body and also death of the spirit. In this case, the death of the body is the same for the righteous as well as the wicked. And the grave is the death of the body of both the righteous and the wicked. On the other hand, the death of the spirit of the wicked makes them captive prisoners, and they are imprisoned in hell. On the other hand, the spirits of the righteous are taken home to the paradise of God. During the resurrection, the bodies will all come forth and be reunited with their spirits from the spirit prison, which is hell, or from the paradise of God. The resurrected beings have perfect knowledge of whatever they did while in life— both the wicked and the righteous. Now man has resurrected from the first death, and he will not die again. Now he is ready to appear at the judgement seat of the Holy One of Israel to be judged of God.

The foregoing teaching of the atonement is as was taught by the Nephi prophet Jacob about 540 BC. During his time about 74 BC, Amulek also taught that the atonement must be infinite. He taught that there was to be a last and great sacrifice, which was to be the Son of God—infinite and eternal. Amulek explained further that this last sacrifice would bring salvation to all believers. It was to bring the bowels of mercy, which overpowers justice. Mercy thus satisfies justice and encircles believers in the arms of safety.

The prophet Alma, who had Amulek for his companion, also taught that the Son of God, the sacrificial lamb, would come to the world to redeem his people and that he would take upon him the transgressions of those who would believe on his name, and that such would have eternal life. Alma taught that the wicked would remain as though there had been no atonement made.

The Nephite prophets spoke and prophesied about future events in much detail. In the New Testament, however, the focus of the account centred around Jesus Christ himself. He knew what he was saying, and the people listened to him. The apostle Paul, who was a latecomer, even with Jesus, is the only one who spoke about spiritual things. He compared the corruptible nature of the living body to the raised incorruptible resurrected body. He talked about the death of Christ loosening the bands of temporal death and stated that all shall be raised from the temporal death and that the body and the spirit shall be reunited. Paul emphasized also that everyone would be resurrected with perfect restoration of body and spirit. And when resurrected, we shall look just as we are in mortality.

Paul says in 1 Corinthians 15:45, "Now, behold, I have spoken unto you concerning the death of the mortal body, and also concerning the resurrection of the mortal body. I say unto you that this mortal body is raised to an immortal body, that is from death, even the first death unto life, that they may die no more, their spirits uniting with their bodies, never to be divided, thus the whole becoming spiritual and immortal, that they can no more see corruption."

It is not easy to say when God completed the organization for the implementation and establishment of the atonement. Statements referring to the foundation of the world indicate that Adam was a living soul. After all, it was Adam's transgression that made the atonement necessary. Further evidence recorded in the book of Alma also demonstrates that Adam and Eve were not alone. The book of Moses sheds more light on the circumstances of Adam and his immediate posterity: "…in exile in the garden of Eden as it were" (Moses 5:12, 13; 6:53–54).

The last two verses quoted above indicate that Adam spoke unto God and was answered that he had been forgiven his transgression in the garden of Eden. This necessarily became big news among the children of Adam. The Son of God had atoned for Adam's guilt. The sins of parents were no more to be answered upon the children. Children are therefore whole from the foundation of the world. God had also concluded that the atonement programme was doable.

The prophet Alma recorded the following, as stated in Alma 12:28–30:

> And after God had appointed that these things should come unto man, behold, then he saw that it was expedient that man should know concerning the things whereof he had appointed unto them. Therefore, he sent angels to converse with them, who caused men to behold of his glory. And they began from that time forth to call upon his name. Therefore, God conversed with men, and made known unto them the plan of redemption, which had been prepared from the foundation of the world; and this He made known unto them according to their faith and their holy works.

The atonement, redemption, and salvation of man answers only the ends of Adam's transgression in the garden of Eden. Sin committed by individuals during this probationary period in mortality is judged according to the book of Revelation 20:12–13 in the New Testament in the Bible.

CHAPTER 4

THE ATONEMENT ORGANIZED

We have been reminded that God sent angels to inform man about the plan of salvation. God made a law for Adam in the beginning and demanded absolute obedience. Infringing the law would attract the death penalty, destroying God's plan to populate the earth. The law was broken. Judgement was pronounced upon Adam, and justice was to take its course, "for dust thou art and unto dust shalt thou return" (Genesis 3:19).

Yet God had said, in Moses 1:39, "For behold, this is my work and my glory —— to bring to pass the immortality and eternal life of man."

God was disappointed in Adam for earning the capital punishment. Yet God needed him to accomplish the programme to populate the earth and bring to pass the immortality and eternal life of man. God needed to redeem this project, and that meant Adam needed to play his inevitable and indispensable role.

God had given a strict law with punishment affixed to it. He had to select an alternative plan for redemption. In that plan, Adam was to be given a probationary period to repent before he died; for he would surely die. God must have had many alternate ways from which to select a suitable change should there be a need for a change. (In the days of Moses, God started with mild plagues, and the severity and intensity of the plagues increased from one to the other until the ultimate plague—death of the firstborn son, which brought Pharaoh and the Egyptian and their armies to their knees. See appendix 1)

God modified the death sentence of Adam by deferring it to a suspended death sentence. The provisions and terms of this period of probation would satisfy justice. It would implement the punishment affixed to the broken law. That would also allow the desire of God for man to live eternally. God, in his wisdom, had a plan. The plan was to have the power to restore the crumbled body and the departed spirit together again. It became necessary that someone else, dearer to the Father than Adam, was to be sacrificed to appease the ends of the law. This was to be a sacrifice for reconciliation or propitiation.

The sacrifice was to reconcile justice and mercy, which was necessary if the man was to be restored back to his perfect form. The sacrificial individual was to have his blood flow out of his body in a manner that would inflict the punishment of pain and misery. An unblemished, sinless person was to sacrifice himself for all Adam's descendants. As soon as his blood touched the ground, the blessing would go as far as the curse was found. The deal would be completed, and the power to effect the resurrection would be in force. Jesus Christ accepted the Father's desire for him to be the sacrificial object. God must have heaved a big sigh of relief when his firstborn son offered himself as a sacrifice for sin.

With the birth of Jesus Christ, there was a misconception, as recorded in 3 Nephi 1:24–25. The belief that it was no longer expedient to observe the law of Moses was soon rectified.

Following the resurrection, Jesus Christ himself taught the Nephites. See 3 Nephi 9:19–22 in the Book of Mormon. Amongst other things, he said, "And ye shall offer up unto me no more the shedding of blood; yea, your sacrifice and your burnt offerings shall be done away, for I will accept none of your sacrifices and your burnt offerings." He also made reference to a statement he made in Israel during his mortal life, as recorded in John 10:16: "And other sheep I have, which are not of this fold; them also I must bring, and they shall hear my voice; and there shall be one-fold, and one shepherd. Therefore, doth my Father love me, because I lay down my life, that I might take it again."

Following the foregoing introductory remarks, we now come to the raison d'être, or the main body, of this presentation. We now come to the establishment of mercy to ameliorate the pain of justice. In the Book of Mormon, the prophet Alma introduces the subject rather gently. He says in Alma 42:15, "And now the plan of mercy could not be brought about except an atonement should be made; therefore, God himself atoneth for the sins of the world, to bring about the plan of mercy, to appease the demands of justice, that God might be a perfect, just God, and a merciful God also."

An atonement became necessary to appease justice and give mercy a chance to bring to pass the immortality and eternal life of man. It would come at the very expensive mercy of a sinless volunteer. This volunteer would suffer an unimaginable punishment of misery and intense pain. It would cause blood to flow through the pores of the skin. Mosiah announced a prophecy of this future event about 124 BC, saying in Mosiah 3:2, 7, "And the things which I shall tell you are made known unto me by an angel from God. And lo, he shall suffer temptations, and pain of body, hunger, thirst, and fatigue, even more than man can suffer, except it be unto death; for behold, blood cometh from every pore, so great shall be his anguish for the wickedness and abominations of his people. And he shall be called Jesus Christ, the Son of God and his mother shall be called Mary." This prophecy was fulfilled in the year AD 33, as recorded by the apostle in Luke 22:44 saying, "And being in agony, he prayed more earnestly; and his sweat was as it were great drops of blood falling down to the ground."

The intense pain and misery would be equal to the everlasting loss of life of man, which is the focus of the bargain. This would appease justice and answer the ends of the broken law. This severe punishment of an innocent, sinless man calls to memory what happened to Job several centuries earlier in mortal life. In this case, Satan, telling lies, accused Job before God.

Again, in chapter 5 of the book of Moses, in the "Pearl of Great Price", the secret combination between Cain and Satan recounts how a sinless and innocent Abel was killed for gain. Cain loved Satan more than God. Satan commanded him, saying, "Make an offering unto the Lord." Abel also made an offering unto the Lord. The Lord had respect unto Abel and his offering.

Satan has thus set a stage for hatred of Cain against his brother Abel, for "Satan knew it and it pleased him." Verses 29 and 30 state that Cain and Satan entered into a covenant in which Satan swore that he would deliver his brother Abel into his hands. And thus Cain entered into a secret combination through which he would murder and get gain. After he slew Abel, he said, "Surely the flocks of my brother falleth into my hands."

Again, in the story of Job, God confirmed with Satan that Job "feareth God, and escheweth evil and still he holdeth fast his integrity" (Job 3:2). God then placed a critical emphasis on

Satan's desires and said, "Although thou movest me against him, to destroy him without course."

Satan's readiness to accuse falsely is hinted at plainly in the book of Revelation 12:10: "…for the accuser who accused them before our God day and night." Satan is a villain and is lawless. The killing of Abel to get gain was murder because it was extra-judicial. It was done out of hatred, envy, and jealousy, and it was for gain. The law of God in Deuteronomy 27:25 says, "Curse is he that taketh reward to slay an innocent person."

Similarly, the punishment of Job was carried out at the insistence of the same villain, Satan. Satan wanted to prove to God that if Job was pushed far enough, Job would be found wanting. It is evident, then, that Cain killed Abel because Satan wanted that to be so. These two examples, in which very sinless and innocent persons, whose righteousness was attested to by God, were punished so severely, even unto death, were extra-judicial.

The atoning sacrifice of Jesus Christ was different. Jesus Christ stood voluntarily as proxy for Adam, who had fallen foul of the law. In this case, a law had been broken, and justice demanded the life of Adam. Adam's death would end God's desire to bring to pass the immortality and eternal life of man. The intervention of Jesus Christ would allow justice to implement the death penalty ultimately. This atonement, which unleashed punishment in the form of severe pain, and even unto death, was a voluntary offer by the sinless, innocent one. The suffering reconciled justice of the law and mercy as God, our Father, had planned for his children. Satan had no part to play in the atoning sacrifice of the Lamb of God. The only credit to him would be his deceitful council to Eve and her husband in the garden of Eden. The atonement was completely legal. A law had been enacted. The law had been infringed upon, and justice took possession of the culprit. A satisfactory punishment was implemented, and both parties, justice and mercy, were satisfied.

The atonement was now organized. It would generate the power needed to restore all things when it was established. It would subdue death. It would undo everything that death had done and effect the resurrection of the dead.

The crumbled remains of man, having disintegrated to become part of Mother Earth, will be reconstituted. The body and the spirit, which had departed, were to be brought together and reunited. The spirit returns to its body, and the body to its spirit, never to be separated again. The power of the atonement, having subdued the power of death, would open the prison gates to set the captives free. The man, thus redeemed, is brought to safety in the hands of mercy to answer the ends of the atonement to bring peace and happiness affixed to the atonement. This brings about a fulfilment of God's desire to bring to pass the immortality and eternal life of man.

Once the plan had been organized, God sent messengers to the earth to announce the good tidings of great joy. The prophet Alma in the Book of Mormon announces this message in Alma 12:28. And he emphasized this and said again in Alma 13:22, "Yea, and the voice of the Lord, and the mouth of angels, doth declare it unto all nations; yea, doth declare it, that they may have glad tidings of great joy; yea and he doth sound these glad tidings among all his people, yea, even to them that are scattered abroad upon the face of the earth; wherefore they have come unto us."

For his role in the plan of redemption and salvation, Jesus Christ, already enjoying the right of the firstborn son, now has authority and power to open the gates of death and hell to free their captive prisoners. Being full of mercy and love, he demands repentance only during the probationary mortal life. Repentance is required for man to have a blissful life after the resurrection. His judgement will take account only of mortal life. Thoughts, words, and actions pertaining to righteousness alone will matter in judgement.

Happily, what results at the end of all these actions will be as follows:

- Justice has not been denied its enforcement of the law.
- Mercy has not been deprived of its role to administer comfort to the embattled soul.

Finally, the body and the spirit are together permanently as the living soul of man. Now man has been redeemed from the fall and has been brought into safety eternally. The plan organized from the foundation of the world was established when our Lord and Redeemer's blood flowed unto the ground at Golgotha. This followed his torment in the garden of Gethsemane. There blood oozed out of the pores of his skin, as intimated by prophecy. The resurrection of the Lamb of God crowned the plan of redemption.

CHAPTER 5

THE FULLNESS OF
THE GOSPEL

The fullness of the gospel makes available everything that needs to be known. It also ensures the information is clearly understood. This would crown God's desire for man to be informed about the plan of redemption. Alma, in the Book of Mormon, discusses the time at which God decided to tell man about his plans. Alma is the only prophet to have mentioned it. Says he in Alma 12: 28–30,

> And after God had appointed that these things should come unto man, behold, then he saw that it was expedient that man should know concerning the things whereof he had appointed unto them; Therefore, He sent angels to converse with them, who caused men to behold of his glory. And they began from that time forth to call upon His name; therefore, God conversed with men, and made known unto them the plan of redemption, which had been prepared from the foundation of the world; and this he made known unto them according to their faith and repentance and their holy works.

In this discussion of the atonement, the author seeks mandate from God—mandate to crown the fullness of the message educating man on this important subject of the atonement of Jesus Christ for the salvation of man. The prayer is that God will give free access to source the information to crown his teaching. God has been disobeyed a number of times in the course of establishing the immortality and eternal life of man. He has had to use alternatives to nullify the negative effects of the disobedience of man. God's first surprise came at the very beginning, when Adam, whom he trusted very much, obeyed Satan and disrupted God's plan. The death of Adam would have to end it all.

Another disappointment came during the time of Noah: "And God saw that the wickedness of man was great in the earth, and that every imagination of the thought of his heart was only evil continually. And it repented the LORD that he had made man on the earth and it grieved him at his heart" (Genesis 6:5–6).

God therefore brought the flood to destroy all but one family of eight souls. Subsequent to the flood, man continued to infuriate God. In the land of Shinar, men planned to build the Tower of Babel, evidently against the wishes of God. This time God relented. He confounded the language which the people had been speaking for more than 1,800 years since Adam (2200 BC). He also dispersed them so that they could no longer plan together contrary to God's wishes. This time there was no loss of life, and the site where the tower was being built was called Babel.

One other example is the meeting of "one's Waterloo." Waterloo is a town in Belgium. On 18 June 1815, Napoleon's main army had an engagement with Wellington's British army at the town. Almost defeated, Wellington prayed for the arrival of the night or the combined German forces of Marshal Gebhard Von Blucher. The British were losing the day bitterly. But just before nightfall, Blucher arrived with 125,000 men. He overturned the misfortune of the British. Just as Babel metamorphosed through Babylon, etc., and has lost its original excitement, so also has Waterloo been forgotten (*Illustrated World Encyclopedia* vol. 20, p. 4858).

After the Tower of Babel was aborted, the language of Jared, his brother (Mahonri Moriancumr), and their families was not confounded. God allowed them to keep the original language used during the building of the tower. This group, now called the Jaredites, remained together with one language. Records show that the brother of Jared had direct, face-to-face communication with the spirit being of Jesus Christ. Jesus Christ appeared to him and gave him the necessary guidelines to travel by sea to a land of promise. The land happens to be America. The last survivor of the Jaredites, one Coriantumr, had the record of the meeting with Jesus Christ, who was yet to be manifested in the flesh.

An introduction to the Jaredite account is found in the book of Omni (Omni 1:12–23) in the Book of Mormon. The last Jaredite prophet, Ether, gave account of the Jaredites. The prophet observed the destruction of the Jaredites in wars. God had warned that they would be destroyed if they continued to be wicked and unrighteous. This property of the Jaredites was given to the people of Zarahemla, who left Jerusalem in 598 BC. The people of Zarahemla—who also left Jerusalem, under the leadership of Mulek—had dwindled in number because of wars. They were found by the people of Mosiah, who were Nephites, descendants of Lehi. Mosiah became king of his own people, the Nephites, and the people of Zarahemla. Their languages were different. After learning each other's languages, both realized they had left Jerusalem at different times. The Nephites left in 600 BC, a few years ahead of Zarahemla and his people. Zarahemla's ancestors had left Jerusalem under the leadership of Mulek in about 587 BC, the year in which Jerusalem was captured. Zedekiah, the king, was taken captive to Babylon. Nebuchadnezzar was king of Babylon from 604–561 BC.

Despite all odds, God achieves his purposes under mysterious circumstances. The accounts of the Jaredites, the people of Zarahemla, and the Nephites are such examples. These accounts confirm that God sent out the atonement message as soon as it was organized. Each of these groups had a prophet leader. Through the leader, God made clear the message of the atonement of Jesus Christ.

The history of the Jaredites and the appearance of Jesus Christ himself before his mortal life is a highly breathtaking and outstanding occurrence. The other two groups received the message through their prophets. One could say that the Jaredites were a great disappointment. What about the Israelites who had him physically and murdered him? We know from 2 Nephi 10:2–10 that the atoning sacrifice would not have happened if the Jews had not been so wicked as to kill one who was evidently their God. The evil one would have loved for the atonement not to happen. The programme and the plan of God for the immortality and eternal life of man would then not have occurred.

THE JAREDITES

Ether, in the Book of Mormon, records that following the abortion of the building of the Tower of Babel, Jared made requests of God. He made the requests through his brother, who was a prophet of God. The brother of Jared thus cried unto the Lord, and the Lord had compassion on Jared. Thus, he did not confound the language of Jared and his brother and their families. God also had compassion on the friends and families of these friends of Jared and his brother, and their language was not confounded.

Also, Jared requested that the Lord send this group whose language had not been confounded from the land of Shinar. Shinar is where the Tower of Babel was aborted. He asked the Lord to send them into a land which was choice above all the earth. The Lord had compassion on Jared again. The Lord asked Jared to gather animals of every kind—male and female—and seeds of every kind, and all those whose language had not been confounded.

The brother of Jared led them to a valley where the Lord would meet Jared. The Lord said, as recorded in Ether 1:42, that he, the Lord, would go before them into the land which was choice above all the earth, and that he would raise there, unto himself, a great nation, and that there would be none greater than that nation of the Jaredites upon all the face of the earth. The Jaredites went to the valley proposed by the Lord, which was called after the mighty Nimrod of the land of Shinar.

The Lord came into the valley of Nimrod and talked to the brother of Jared, and he led them into the wilderness. They built barges, with which they crossed many waters. The Lord warned about the land of promise, which was to be their destination. Whoever would possess it would serve God or would be swept off in the fullness of his wrath. The Jaredites were told in Ether 2:12 that Jesus Christ was the God of the Promised Land and that they were to serve him. The Jaredites finally came to the sea at a place they called Morriancumr, and they dwelt in tents at the seashore for four years. The Lord called the brother of Jared to build barges as he had done previously. The brother of Jared requested the Lord to provide light and air in the barges. The Lord asked him for ideas to help them live in the barges, as they would be under the waves of the sea at times.

As we read in chapter 3 of the book of Ether, the brother of Jared made eight vessels. He then went into an exceedingly high mountain and cut sixteen small transparent stones out of a rock. He held these stones up in his hands and prayed, saying in Ether 3:4–6,

> ...therefore touch these stones, O Lord, with thy finger, and prepare them that they may shine forth in darkness; in the vessels which we have prepared, that we may have light while we shall cross the sea... behold, the Lord stretched forth his hand and touched the stones one by one with his finger. And the veil was taken from the eyes of the brother of Jared, and he saw the finger of the Lord; and it was as the finger of a man like unto flesh and blood; and the brother of Jared fell down before the Lord, for he was struck with fear.

The Lord conversed with him briefly in 13–16:

> And when he had said these words, behold, the Lord showed himself and said: Because thou knowest these things ye are redeemed from the fall; therefore, ye are brought back into my presence. Behold, I am he who was prepared from the foundation of the world to redeem my people. Behold, I am Jesus Christ, I am the Father and the Son. In me shall all mankind have life, and that

eternally, even they who shall believe on my name:
and they shall become my sons and daughters.
And never have I shown myself unto man whom I
have created, for never has man believed in me as
thou hast. Seest thou that ye are created after my
own image? Yea, even all men were created in the
beginning after my own image. Behold, this body,
which ye now behold, is the body of my spirit; and
even as I appear unto thee to be in the spirit will I
appear unto my people in the flesh.

This interaction is similar to when the Lord showed
himself unto the Nephites. See 3 Nephi, 11:8–16 in the Book
of Mormon.

The Jaredites lived for many generations, but they
perished because they disobeyed God. The last Jaredite, one
Corriantumr, died nine months after he had been seen by the
people of Zarahemla. The Lord administered to the Jaredites.
He did same with the Nephites, who followed many centuries
afterwards. The two groups did not know each other. They
landed far apart in different places on the American continent.

The Jaredites, the people of Zarahemla, and the Nephites
landed separately at different locations in their own times on the
American continent. These three major groups were led by very
trusted men, and their people might have been righteous in the
sight of the Lord. These are the people that the Lord planned
to send to this land, which is choice above all other lands and
which is now called America. From one generation to the other,
the Jaredites progressed when they were righteous. When they
were wicked and disobeyed God, they suffered disaster and
wars. The last two Jaredites were Shiz and Corriantumr. They
assembled all the people in two groups and brought them to
the last mortal combat until only Corriantumr remained. There

had been slain two million mighty men, and also their wives and children. God spoke to Ether, the last prophet, who was secluded from this last battle, and said unto him,

> Go forth. And he went forth, and beheld that the words of the Lord had all been fulfilled; and he finished his record. Now the last words which were written by Ether were these: whether the Lord will that I be translated, or that I suffer the will of the Lord in the flesh, it mattereth not, if it so be that I am saved in the kingdom of God. Amen. (Ether 15:23–24)

THE NEPHITES

(And the Atonement message)

According to Ether 6:11–12 in the Book of Mormon, the Jaredites travelled in their barges for 344 days. The record shows also that the friends of Jared and his brother numbered about twenty-two. They also had sons and daughters before they came to the Promised Land. The number of the sons and daughters of the brother of Jared in his old age were twenty–two. The number of the sons and daughters of Jared were twelve, including four sons. The brother of Jared saw Jesus Christ (his spirit body) in full daylight when they were travelling on land in preparation to set off by sea.

Lehi, however, left Jerusalem with his wife and four sons. They went with his friend Ishmael and his family together with one other man, Zoram. They arrived at the shores of the Red Sea after eight years of travel by land. Nephi, the fourth son, who became the leader of this group, built a ship. Lehi had two other sons, Jacob and Joseph, during their travel. They crossed by sea to the Promised Land. This was the same continent where the Jaredites landed and were destroyed by their wars. In the Book of Mormon, Nephi says, "And I, Nephi, do not make a full account of the things which my father hath written, for he hath written many things which he saw in visions and in dreams" (1 Nephi 1:16).

The Lord spoke to Nephi, and he was chosen to rule over his brethren. 1 Nephi 2:20 explains that so long as they kept the Lord's commandments, they would prosper and be led to a land of promise which had been prepared for them and which was choice above all the lands. The summary of 1 Nephi 10 tells of a Messiah, a Saviour or a Redeemer, among the Jews. Lehi tells about the death and resurrection of the Messiah, the Lamb of God, who should take away the sins of the world.

In 2 Nephi 2, Lehi teaches that redemption comes in and through the Holy Messiah and that he offers himself as a sacrifice for sin to answer the ends of the law, unto all those who have a broken heart and a contrite spirit. Enmity between the two factions of Lehi's family deepened. And as recorded in 2 Nephi 2:5, the family was divided, with Nephi separating himself. Going along with Nephi and his family were Zoram and his family; Sam, Nephi's elder brother, and his family; Jacob and Joseph, his younger brothers; and also his sisters and all those who would go with him. After many days of travel in the wilderness, they came to a place which they called Nephi. And they were called the people of Nephi. He also had the records on plates of brass and the ball called Liahona. Thirty years after departure from Jerusalem, Nephi ordained Jacob and Joseph priests and teachers.

As recorded in 2 Nephi 9, Jacob taught mightily, referring to the records of Isaiah which they had with them.

> Yea, I know that ye know that in the body he
> shall show himself unto those at Jerusalem, from

whence we came; for it is expedient that it should be among them; for it behoveth the great Creator that he sufferth himself to be subject unto man in the flesh, and die for all men, that all men might become subject unto him. For as death had passed upon all men, to fulfill the merciful plan of the great creator, there must needs be a power of resurrection, and the resurrection must needs come unto man by reason of the fall; and the fall came by reason of transgression; and because man became fallen they were cut off from the presence of the Lord.

The Nephites, during their time, had several prophets who preached the atonement of Jesus Christ. The accounts of the Jaredites, including the communication with Jesus Christ about 2,600 years earlier, were available to Moroni in AD 421. These accounts had been recorded by the last Jaredite prophet, Ether. The records got into the hands of Moroni. Moroni was the last surviving Nephite warrior. As the angel Moroni, he worked with the prophet Joseph Smith in the 1830s to lay the foundation of the Church of Jesus Christ Of Latter-day Saints in this dispensation of the fullness of time.

CHAPTER 6

FOUNDATION OF
THE WORLD

According to Mosiah 4:6 in the Book of Mormon, the atonement has been prepared from the foundation of the world. Scientific reports in *The Illustrated World Encyclopedia*, volume 7, page 1727, indicate that the earth is one of several planets known to man. These reports state that the sun and its planets, including the earth, may have been formed about five billion years ago. Many changes have taken place since the formation of the sun and its planets. At first the earth was so hot that nothing could live on it. Initially there was no water but only hot gases surrounding the entire globe.

Millions of years later, some of the gases cooled and made water that then covered all of the earth. The most important change in the earth occurred late in its history. About a million years ago, the earth became very much like it is today, except there were great sheets of ice called glaciers. It is believed that the earth was in existence millions of years before Adam was planted thereon. This planet, Earth, on which human life has developed, including all people and their ways of life, is known as the world. Without man on the earth, there was no world, but only the earth.

It is estimated that Adam's day was about 4,000 years before the day of Jesus Christ. However, no one knows how old Adam was when he disobeyed God and ate the forbidden fruit. This disobedience caused man to be ostracized from before the presence of God.

Whom shall I send?

It is believed that God needed a representative to teach man on earth to make informed choices. Those who would make correct choices after they had been educated by the ambassador of God would enter into the rest of God. The ambassador was going to teach as the master teacher, a rabbi. Man was then to be judged and graded in various degrees after judgement. Then man would be assigned their deserved kingdoms—the celestial, terrestrial, and teletial kingdoms.

However, a new dimension came into play at the foundation of the world when Adam committed blunders by disobeying the law.

Atonement then became necessary to salvage the man in the plan of salvation if God's plan for man was to be achieved. This became a necessary addition to the education that was to help the man to make informed choices. The plan of salvation, the ultimate component of which is the atonement of Jesus Christ, could not have started before the fall of Adam. The fall made the atonement necessary. Of necessity, God must have spent a day or two putting together the redeeming plan for which atonement was a necessary requirement.

The new strategy established a merciful appeasement to release Adam from permanent death. Adam thus could live again after the death pronounced in the garden of Eden had been executed. The crowning event was the killing of a sacrificial lamb. The killing of the lamb in the person of Jesus Christ was essential for reconciliation. Jesus was to be killed in an unusual, painful, and disgraceful way. Following the death. Jesus's spirit and body were to reunite inseparably again in the process called "the resurrection of the dead".

For those three days in death, the spirit of Jesus Christ would remain disembodied. During that time, he would go to the spirit world, as we learn in 1 Peter 3:19 and 1 Peter 4:16. His body would await unification with the spirit, which would occur in due time.

RESURRECTION

During those three days, power would emanate from the atoning sacrifice. Jesus Christ would be killed as an unblemished, sinless sacrificial lamb to answer the end of the sin of Adam. This power would answer the ends of the atonement to establish the gains affixed to the atoning sacrifice. Each sacrifice brings certain blessings. The greater the sacrifice is, the more elaborate the blessings. Immediately with the maturation and establishment of this power, which is the blessing affixed to the sacrifice of Jesus Christ to reconcile justice and grace, the Lord would arise as a resurrected being. This power would effect the resurrection of the dead.

The atonement of the blood of Jesus Christ invokes the power of the resurrection of the dead. The power of the resurrection of the dead brings back the dust from the earth to reconstitute the living soul. Restoring everything perfectly, the departed spirit is recalled. The spirit and the body reunite, never again to be separated. The man is thus restored into the presence of God. The power of the resurrection nullifies the strength of hell and the sting of death. Hell is the spirit prison, and death is the grave.

This power has given man victory over hell and the grave.

And so it is now that, through Jesus Christ, God the Father has given us victory over death. The reconciliatory atoning sacrifice has brought us out of condemnation and into freedom.

> And after God had appointed that these things should come unto man, behold, then he saw that it was expedient that man should know concerning the things whereof he had appointed unto them. Therefore, he sent angels to converse with them, who caused men to behold of his glory. (Alma 12:28–29)

The quote above presupposes that Adam and Eve were not alone. They may have had many descendants who needed reassurance. The organization of the plan to redeem man following the fall must have taken quite a while. Despite the fall, the procreation programme, probably established when Adam was created, must have been working. Now that the organization of the redemption was complete, its establishment and implementation a foregone conclusion, God needed to reassure Adam's posterity of a glorious future. Its establishment, however, would wait until the death of Jesus Christ, about 4,000 years after Adam. The year of Adam (AM) 1 equals 4,000 BC (the years before Jesus Christ.)

The message reached Adam almost immediately, according to Moses 5: 6–9 in the Book of Mormon.

And again, in Moses 6:52–54, Adam is told that

> If Adam would turn unto God, and harken unto his voice, and believe, and repent of his transgressions, and be baptized, even in water, in the name of the Only Begotten Son, who is full of grace and truth, which is Jesus Christ, the only name which shall be given under heaven, whereby

salvation shall come unto the children of men, Adam would receive the gift of the Holy Ghost, asking all things in his name, and whatsoever Adam shall ask it shall be given him. Behold, Adam's transgression is forgiven in the Garden of Eden. There was popular saying among the people, that the Son of God had atoned for the original guilt, wherein the sin of the parents cannot be answered upon the heads of the children for they are whole from the foundation of the world.

Here now follows an encyclopaedic chronological review of some of the writings of the prophets. These prophets were part of the chain of messengers of God. They carried the message about the things God had appointed unto man. According to chapter five of the book of Moses, the Pearl of Great Price, Adam and Eve had children who had begun to multiply and replenish the earth. God spoke to Adam and asked him to offer sacrifices unto the Lord. Adam was obedient this time, and he offered sacrifices unto the Lord. An angel of the Lord educated Adam, saying in verses 7 and 9,

> The sacrifice was a similitude of the sacrifice of the Only Begotten of the Father, which is full of grace and truth… And in that day Adam spoke Messianically saying: I am the Only Begotten of the Father from the beginning, henceforth and forever, that as you have fallen you may be redeemed, and all mankind, even as many as will.

Adam and Eve had Cain and his younger brother Abel before Seth, who was born when Adam was 130 years old. The year of Adam when he became a living soul is estimated to be 4,000 BC. We shall follow the history from this date till AD

1, when Jesus Christ was born, with some quotations and dates as much as possible.

Following the interaction between the angel and Adam quoted before; the earliest quotation is Moses 7:47: "And behold, Enoch saw the day of the coming of the Son of man, even in the flesh; and his soul rejoiced, saying: The righteous is lifted up, and the Lamb is slain from the foundation of the world; and through faith I am in the bosom of the Father, and behold, Zion is with me."

Enoch was translated at the age of 365 years, in the year of Adam 987, which is BC 3013. "And it came to pass that Enoch saw the day of the coming of the Son of man in righteousness for the space of a thousand years" (Moses 7:65).

From Enoch's prophecy, we come to relatively recent times, starting in Israel with the prophet Hosea, who started prophesying in the year 790 BC. Hosea's prophesy refers to the baby Jesus in his sojourn to Egypt. "When Israel was a child, I loved him, and called my son out of Egypt" (Hosea 11:1).

The second prophet quoted in this work is Isaiah, a prophet in Jerusalem between 740–701 BC. Most of Isaiah's prophecies deal with the coming of the Redeemer. He prophesied that Christ, as God, would be born into mortality by a virgin and would be among the people to save and redeem them. He says in Isaiah 7:14, "Therefore, the Lord himself shall give you a sign; Behold, a virgin shall conceive and bear a son and shall call his name Immanuel." He says also in Isaiah 9:6, "For unto us a child is born, unto us a son is given… and his name shall be called Wonderful, Counselor the Prince of Peace."

Isaiah spoke messianically, saying in Isaiah 42:6–7, "I the LORD have called thee in righteousness, and will hold thine hand, and will keep thee, and give thee for a covenant of the people, for a light of the Gentiles; To open the blind eyes, to bring out the prisoners from the prison, and them that sit in darkness out of the prison house."

The prophet Micah prophesied from 722 BC and said in 1 Micah 5:2, "But thou, Bethlehem Ephratah, though thou be little among the thousands of Judah, yet out of thee shall He come forth unto me that is to be ruler in Israel..."

The prophet Daniel was carried away as a captive in 609 BC. Nevertheless, in Daniel chapter 9 it is recorded that the angel Gabriel revealed to Daniel the coming of the Messiah, which was to make reconciliation for iniquity.

While in America, the prophet Nephi in the Book of Mormon testified that there were many prophets in Jerusalem during the time of Daniel. Nephi told of his father's, Lehi's, prophecy while in Jerusalem about the coming of the Messiah and also the redemption of the world. Also, he prophesied that 600 years from the time his father left Jerusalem, a prophet would be raised up among the Jews. In other words this person would be a Messiah who was to be the Saviour of the world.

He says in 1 Nephi 1:4, "...they must repent, or the great city of Jerusalem must be destroyed." Nephi records in 1 Nephi 1:19 that "Lehi prophesied the coming of Messiah, and also the redemption of the world."

Therefore, from 600 BC, the prophets were giving dates regarding the precise time of the coming of the redeemer of the world. More details of the Lord and his birth began to be given by prophesy. Nephi recorded again about 598 BC. In 1 Nephi 11:7, it is stated that Nephi saw in a vision the Virgin Mother and the Son of God and his apostles. 1 Nephi 19:7–8 also states that Nephi saw in a vision the suffering and crucifixion of the Lamb of God.

Just about this time, when Nephi was receiving messages about the redeemer, it was recorded in Ezekiel 37 in the Old

Testament that Ezekiel was asked to prophesy for restoration of the dead in the valley of dry bones. He also prophesied, speaking messianically, "Behold, O my people, I will open your graves and cause you to come up out of your graves."

Continuing his instructions to his son Jacob, Lehi said in 2 Nephi 2:6–7, "Wherefore redemption cometh in and through the Holy Messiah; for he is full of grace and truth. Behold he offereth himself a sacrifice for sin, to answer the ends of the law, unto all those who have a broken heart and a contrite spirit; and unto none else can the ends of the law be answered."

According to Nephi's prophecies, the role of the Messiah as the sacrificial Lamb of God was not to fail under any circumstances. God provided a surety for the success of his sacrifice. He says in 2 Nephi 10:3–5 (about 550 BC), "Wherefore, as I said unto you, it must needs be expedient that Christ – should come among the Jews, among those who are the more wicked part of the world; and they shall crucify him — for thus it behooveth our God, and there is none other nation on earth that would crucify their God. But because of priestcrafts and iniquities, they at Jerusalem will stiffen their necks against him that he be crucified."

We also read the following in 2 Nephi 26:28–29: "The Lord commanded that there shall be no priestcraft; "For, behold, priestcrafts are that men preach and set themselves up for a light unto the world, that they may get gain and praise of the world; but they seek not the welfare of Zion."

Nephi's prophecies occurred during the period BC 559–545, and in 2 Nephi 25:13, he states, "Behold, they will crucify him; and after he is laid in a sepulcher for the space of three days he shall rise from the dead, with healing in his wings; and all those who shall believe on his name shall be saved in the kingdom of God."

Nephi says again in 2 Nephi 25:19, "For according to the words of the prophets, the Messiah cometh in six hundred years from the time that my father left Jerusalem — his name shall be called Jesus Christ, the son of God."

During the period BC 148–120, a descendant of Nephi called Mosiah was king of the Nephites. He also contributed to disseminating the message from God. He says in Mosiah 16:8, 15,

> But there is a resurrection, therefore the grave hath no victory, and the sting of death is swallowed up in Christ... Teach them that redemption cometh through Christ the Lord, who is the very Eternal Father. Amen.

Another Nephite prophet, Alma, functioned during the period 91–52 BC. He prophesied, saying in Alma 7:10, "And behold, he shall be born of Mary, at Jerusalem which is the land of our fathers, she being a virgin, a precious and chosen vessel, who shall be overshadowed and conceived by the power of the Holy Ghost, and bring forth a son, yea, even the Son of God."

In the year BC 6, Samuel, the Lamanite prophet, journeyed to the Nephites and prophesied unto them. Helaman 14:2 in the Book of Mormon states, "Behold, I give unto you a sign; for five years more cometh, and behold, then cometh the Son of God to redeem all those who shall believe on his name."

Samuel the Lamanite continued his prophecy in Helaman 14:16–17, saying, "Yea, behold, this death bringeth to pass the resurrection, and redeemeth all mankind from the first death — that spiritual death; for all mankind, by the fall of Adam being cut off from the presence of the Lord, are considered as dead, both as to things temporal and to things spiritual. But behold, the resurrection of Christ redeemeth mankind, yea, even all mankind, and bringeth them back into the presence of the Lord."

According to Helaman 14:16, the fall of Adam, which was the first death, was also a spiritual death. This is because the fall of Adam cut off mankind from the presence of the Lord. Man is thus considered dead both temporally and spiritually.

Now, with respect to Israel, Jesus Christ repeatedly said, (as in 3 Nephi 9:16), "I came unto my own and my own received me not. And the scriptures concerning my coming are fulfilled."

As also in the Gospel of John 1:11 and Doctrine and Covenant 6:21, The Gospel of Luke says the following in Luke 1:27–28, 40–46:

> And in the sixth month (of Elizabeth's conception) the angel Gabriel was sent from God unto a city in Galilee named Nazareth, to a virgin espoused to a man whose name was Joseph of the house of David; and the virgin's name was Mary. And the angel came in unto her, and said, Hail, thou that are favoured, the Lord is with thee: blessed art thou among women… And entered into the house of Zacharias, and saluted Elizabeth. And it came to pass, that, when Elizabeth heard the salutation of Mary, the babe leaped in her womb; and Elizabeth was filled with the Holy Ghost. And she spake with a loud voice, and said, blessed are thou among women, and blessed is the fruit of thy womb. And whence is this to me that the mother of my Lord should come to me? And Mary said, my soul doth magnify the Lord, And my spirit hath rejoiced in God my Saviour. And Mary abode with her about three months, and returned to her home.

The foregoing scriptures, quoted liberally, illustrate that the message of the birth of the Lord, Jesus Christ, was published not only in his land of birth but also abroad, by the prophets in their various locations across the world.

In the Year of Our Lord AD 1

The following is recorded in the Gospel of Luke 2:4, 6:

> And Joseph also went up from Galilee, out of the city of Nazareth, into Judea, unto the city of David, which is called Bethlehem. And so it was, that, while they were there, the days were accomplished that she should be delivered.

Nephi recounts his experiences during the time when the days were accomplished that Mary should be delivered. He says in 3 Nephi 1:12–14,

> And it came to pass that he cried mightily unto the Lord all that day; and behold, the voice of the Lord came unto him, saying; Lift up your head and be of good cheer; for behold, the time is at hand, and on this night shall be the sign, *and* on the morrow come I into the world, to show unto the world that I will fulfill all that which I have caused to be spoken by the mouth of my holy prophets. Behold, I come unto my own, to fulfill all things which I have made known unto the children of men from the foundation of the world, and to do the will, both of the Father and of the Son — of the Father because of me, and of the Son because of my flesh. And behold, the time is at hand, and this night will the sign be given.

At this time, the spirit was in heaven and the body from the dust was struggling with the mother in labour at birthing time. His record continues:

> And it came to pass that the words which came unto Nephi were fulfilled, according as they have been spoken; for behold, at the going down of the sun there was no darkness; and the people began to be astonished because there was no darkness when the night came. And there were many, who had not believed the words of the prophets, and who fell to the earth and became as though they were dead, for they knew that the great plan of destruction which they had laid for those who believed in the words of the prophets had been frustrated; for the sign which had been given was already at hand. And they began to know that the son of God must shortly appear, yea, in fine, all the people upon the face of the whole earth from the west to the east, both in the land north and in the land south, were so exceedingly astonished that they fell to the earth. For they knew that the prophets had testified of these things for many years, and that the sign which had been given was already at hand; and they began to fear because of their iniquity and their unbelief. And it came to pass that there was no darkness in that night, but it was as light as though it was mid-day. And it came to pass that the sun did rise in the morning again, according to its proper order; and they knew that, it was the day that the Lord should be born, because of the sign which had been given. And it had come to pass, yea, all things, every whit, according to the words of the prophets. And it came to pass also that a new star did appear, according to the word. (3 Nephi 1:14–21)

The Nephites in the Promised Land in America relied only on the fulfilment of the prophecy, which unfolded before their eyes. The Jews in Israel, however, viewed as physical the occurrence of the birth of the Lord. It is recorded in the Gospel of Luke 2:7–14:

> And she brought forth her first born son. And there were in the same country shepherds abiding in the fields, keeping watch over the flock by night. And, lo, the angel of the Lord came upon them, and they were sore afraid. And the angel said unto them, fear not: for, behold, I bring good tidings of great joy, which shall be for all people. For unto you is born this day in the city of David a Saviour, which is Christ the Lord. And this shall be a sign unto you: Ye shall find a babe wrapped in swaddling clothes, lying in a manger. And suddenly there was with the angel a multitude of heavenly hosts praising God, and saying, Glory to God in the highest, and on earth peace, goodwill toward men.

Having observed the fulfilment of the prophecy of the birth of the Lord, some of the Nephites claimed that the law of Moses had been fulfilled and was to be done away with. However, the third book of Nephi says,

> And there were no contentions; save it was a few that began to preach, endeavoring to prove by the scriptures that it was no more expedient to observe the law of Moses. Now in this thing they did err, having not understood the scriptures. But it came to pass that they soon became converted, and were convinced of the error which they were in, for it was made known unto them that the law was not yet fulfilled, and that it must be fulfilled in every whit;

yea, the word came to them that it must be fulfilled; yea, that one jot or tittle should not pass away till it should all be fulfilled; therefore, in this same year were they brought to a knowledge of their error and did confess their faults. (3 Nephi 1:24–25)

CHAPTER 7

JESUS CHRIST AS PREMORTAL BEING

P remortal Jesus Christ could be said to be ubiquitous. This is because he was everywhere and in all things. And as the apostle John writes in the Gospel of John 1:1–3, "In the beginning was the Word, and the Word was with God, and the Word was God. The same was in the beginning with God. All things were made by him; and without him was not anything made that was made."

When God said in Genesis 1:26, "Let us make man in our image, after our likeness", Jesus Christ was with the Father. When he appeared to the Brother of Jared in the Spirit Being about 2,400 BC, he said, "Behold, I am Jesus Christ, I am the Father and the Son" (Ether 3:14). Also, the prophet Abinadi taught in Mosiah 15:34, in the Book of Mormon, that he would be called the Father because he was conceived by the power of God and the Son, because of the flesh, thus becoming the Father and the Son.

The Jaredites, the people of Zarahemla, and the Nephites were told, as recorded in the Book of Mormon, that Jesus Christ, then a spirit being, was the God of the Promised Land. He is also known and referred to as the God of Israel. The people of Israel killed their God when He came to his own and his own received him not. Sometimes it is not easy to determine whether the appellation "the Father", or "God", or "the Very Eternal God" refers to Jesus Christ or his Father, who is our Father also. Knowing that the Father and the Son are separate beings and also are the major constituents of the Godhead, will suffice to put this fine tuning between the Father and the Son to rest. For after all, Jesus himself says in John 10:30, "I and my Father are one."

JESUS CHRIST IN MORTAL LIFE

The apostle John's testimony of Jesus Christ in mortal life is summed up briefly in John 21:25: "And there are also many other things which Jesus did, the which, if they were all to be written everyone, I suppose that even the whole world could not contain the books that should be written. Amen."

The above testimony of John is perfectly true, and this work will not scratch even the tip of the tip of the iceberg. Having received many of the prophecies about the coming of Jesus Christ, it is now time to follow the fulfilment of the prophecy in his mortal life. The evidence of the birth of Jesus Christ was covered in the previous chapter. We now continue with events following his birth in the year AD 1.

It is recorded in the gospel of Luke 2:21–22, 25–32 as follows:

> And when eight days were accomplished for the circumcision of the child, his name was called Jesus, which was so named of the angel before he was conceived in the womb. And when the days of her purification according to the Law of Moses were

accomplished, they brought him to Jerusalem, to
present him to the Lord... And, behold, there was a
man in Jerusalem, whose name was Simeom... And
it was revealed unto him by the Holy Ghost, that he
should not see death, before he had seen the Lord's
Christ. And he came by the Spirit into the temple
and when the parents brought in the child Jesus, to
do for him after the custom of the law. Then took
he him up in his arms, and blessed God, and said...
Lord, now lettest thou thy servant departs in peace,
according to thy word: For my eyes have seen thy
salvation, which thou hast prepared before the face
of all people; A light to lighten the Gentiles, and the
glory of thy people Israel.

King Herod, an Idumaean and thus a descendant of Esau,
allied himself with the patriotic party of the Jews. Hearing of
the birth of Jesus Christ, who by prophecy was the King of the
Jews, Herod concluded that Jesus was the "stone on which he
was to fall or else overleap." Herod thus planned to take the
life of the baby Jesus by strategy. This is recorded in Matthew
2:12, 14–15:

>And being warned of God in a dream that they
>should not return to Herod, they (wise men from
>the east) departed unto their own country another
>way. And when they were departed behold the angel
>of the LORD appeared to Joseph in a dream saying,
>"Arise and take the young child and his mother, and
>flee into Egypt, and be thou there until I bring thee
>word; for Herod will seek the young child to destroy
>him. When he arose he took the young child and his
>mother by night, and departed into Egypt.

The family remained there until Herod died. It was then

fulfilled, which was spoken of the Lord by the prophet saying, "Out of Egypt have I called my son." **Matthew 2:15.**

> But when Herod died, an angel of the Lord appeared in a dream to Joseph in Egypt. The angel asked Joseph to take the young child and his mother and go into the land of Israel; for those who sought the young child's life were dead. Saying, Arise, and take the young child and his mother, and go into the land of Israel: for they are dead which sought the young child's life. And he arose, and took the young child and his mother, and came into the land of Israel. (Matthew 2:19–21)

The apostle John predicted by revelation this episode in the early life of the infant Jesus Christ, as recorded in Revelation 12:4–6, which reveals Satan's plan for the destruction of the infant Jesus. Of course, the plan for the Atonement could not be nipped in the bud.

> … and the dragon stood before the woman which was ready to be delivered for to devour her child as soon as he was born. And she brought forth a man child, who was to rule the nations with the rod of iron: and her child was caught up unto God and to his throne. And the woman fled into the wilderness, where she had a place prepared of God, that they should feed her there a thousand two hundred and three score days. (Revelation 12:4–6)

No more was heard of the child Jesus until the events recorded in Luke 2:42–47: "And when he was 12 years old they went to Jerusalem after the custom of the feast. The parents could not find him after the feast for three days. They then found him in the temple sitting in the mist of the doctors, both hearing them, and asking them questions. And all that heard him were astonished that he understood the doctors and gave impressive answers to their questions."

From the time he reached the age of twelve years, the scriptures are silent about Jesus Christ. He resurfaces at AD 30 till his death in AD 34. John the Baptist was the first to make the people aware of the presence of the Lord. This is recorded in John 1:20: "And John the Baptist, confessed and denied not; but he confessed and said that he was not the Christ."

John was baptizing in Bethabara beyond Jordan, and Jesus was standing among those ready to be baptized. John made them to understand that Jesus was his superior, but he never saw him. He was baptizing with water and working to introduce Jesus to Israel. John testified that Jesus was the Son of God.

This was the period of expectation of the Messiah, and there appeared to be networks of interested people looking out for the Messiah. Two of John's disciples who heard him speak followed Jesus. One of the two who followed Jesus was Andrew, Simon Peter's brother.

He looked for his own brother, Simon Peter, and informed him that they had found the Messiah—in other words, the Christ.

Philip also looked for Nathaniel and informed him that they had found him of whom Moses, in the law, and the prophets wrote—Jesus of Nazareth, the son of Joseph. Nathaniel retorted, "Can there any good thing come out of Nazareth?" Phillip invited Nathaniel to come and see for himself. "Nathaniel answered and said unto him, Rabbi, thou art the Son of God; thou art the King of Israel" (John 1:49).

It is recorded that Jesus was going to Galilee through Samaria, and he came to the city of Sychar, and Jacob's well was there. He interacted with a woman at the well of Jacob in the Gospel of John, chapter 4:25. The woman said unto him,

> I know that Messiah cometh, which is called Christ: when he is come, he will tell us all things. Jesus saith unto her, I that speak unto thee am he… The woman then left her water pot, and went her way into the city, and said to the men. Come, see a man, which told me all things that ever I did: is not this the Christ? Then they went out of the city, and came unto him… And many more believed because of his own word. And said unto the woman, now we believe, not because of thy saying: for we have heard him ourselves, and know that this is indeed the Christ; the Saviour of the world. (John 4:25–26, 28–30, 41–42)

And many of the people believed in Christ and wondered if any other person apart from the Christ could do such miracles. He exorcised many with devils who were crying and saying, "Thou art Christ the Son of God." Jesus rebuked them and asked them to shut up.

> Jesus and his group arrived at the country of the Gadarenes which is over against Galilee. And on arrival a certain man from the city met him. He had been possessed by devils for a long time, and wore no clothes, neither did he live in any house, but lived rather in the tombs.

> When he saw Jesus, he cried out, and fell down before him, and with a loud voice said, what have I to do with thee, Jesus, thou Son of God most high? I beseech thee, torment me not. (Luke 8:26–28)

Now we know that many people received the message that a Saviour of the World—a Christ, a Messiah—would be born. His birth was to make reconciliation to answer the ends of a broken law. The living, the dead and evil spirits, and Satan and his angels all recognized that this would happen. There was a network of people who searched for the Christ even though Christ was with them. They did not know him until John the Baptist said, "Behold the Lamb of God, which taketh away the sin of the world." **John 1:29.** The Lord had to walk the length of the rope to fulfil the purposes for which the Father sent him. Now there came the advent, with a fulfilment of all the expectations emanating from the many prophecies from the time of Adam. The time had arrived for the sinless to suffer severe punishment. The punishment was equal to punishment for the sin of all men who will populate the earth from Adam to the end of time.

When the authorities want to arrest people deemed "wanted", they are more vigilant during festive occasions. The Passover was a great festive period. Many travellers would go home to Jerusalem for the celebration.

And so it was as stated in Matthew 26:

> … the first day of the feast of the unleavened the disciples came to the Lord, saying unto him; Where will thou that we prepare for thee to eat the Passover?… Now when the even was come, he sat down with the twelve. And as they did eat, he said, verily I say unto you, that one of you shall betray me… The Son of man goeth as it is written of him: but woe unto that man by whom the son of man is betrayed! It had been good for that man if he had not been born. (Matthew 26:17, 20–21, 24)

Could this have been said of the nation Israel? Is this nearly similar to 2 Nephi 10:3–7? This time was in the year AD 34, and most probably in April.

Mathew 26:30 states, "And when they had sung a hymn, they went out into the Mount of Olives."

Matthew 26:36–37 records that Jesus went with them to a place called Gethsemane and asked the disciples to sit and wait while he went further to pray. And he took with him Peter, and the two brothers James and John. He was very sad with a heavy heart. Jesus separated himself from the disciples for a considerable time and prayed.

Matthew 26:45–47 states that he came back to his disciples and asked them to sleep and rest; time was up and the son of man is betrayed into the hands of sinners. He asked the disciples to be ready to leave because the betrayer was close. "And while he yet spake, lo, Judas one of the twelve came and with him a great multitude with swords and staves, from the chief priest and elders of the people" (Matthew 26:47).

To the disciple who struck the servant of the high priests and smote off his ear, Jesus, rebuking him, said, "Thinketh thou that I cannot now pray to my Father, and He shall presently give me more than twelve legions of angels? But how then shall the scriptures be fulfilled that thus it must be" (Matthew 26:53–54)

Following up on these questions by Jesus Christ, the next reasonable questions should be as follows:

- Was Judas Iscariot wrong in bringing the soldiers to take Jesus away?
- Should he have allowed prevention of the atoning sacrifice?

Many things were done in order that the scriptures and

prophesies of the prophets be fulfilled. Judas Iscariot's role that he played was in furtherance of the fulfilment of the atoning sacrifice, which was due to take place a day or two later. This question has the background that all the prophets were given their messages from Jesus himself, who was their God. "In the same Hour said Jesus to the multitudes, are ye come out as against a thief with swords and staffs for to take me, I sat daily with you teaching in the temple, and ye laid no hold of me. But all this was done, that the scriptures of the prophets might be fulfilled" (Matthew 26:55–57, 59).

The messengers took Jesus to Caiaphas, the high priest, around whom the scribes and the elders were assembled. "Now the chief priest and the elders and all the council, sought false witness against Jesus to put him to death" (Matthew 26:59).

And as Jesus answered, the high priest put pressure on him to say whether he was the Christ, the Son of God. Of course, Jesus would not deny this. "Jesus answered and said unto him; thou hast said, nevertheless I say unto you, Hereafter shall ye see the son of man, sitting on the right hand of power, and coming in the clouds of heaven" (Matthew 26:64).

For what Jesus said, he was found guilty of blasphemy, judged to be guilty, and sentenced to death. And they started to mock him and humiliate him. This period was the very beginning of the very humiliating and painful sacrifice for reconciliation. Jesus Christ was the propitiation for the reconciliation. All this happened on Thursday, going deep into the night. "When the morning was come, all the Chief Priests and elders of the people took counsel against Jesus to put him to death" (Matthew 27:1).

Finally, Pilate, the governor, released Jesus to be killed, according to the pressure of the mobs at the court. The whole band of soldiers mocked him and led him away to crucify him.

"Now from the sixth hour, there was darkness over all the land unto the ninth hour when Jesus cried with a loud voice, saying, My God, My God, why hast thou forsaken me? Jesus, when he had cried again with a loud voice, yielded up the ghost" (Matthew 27:45, 50.)

Other records of the gospel recorded the death of Jesus. Mark 15:25–26 and 33–34 also confirm the mortal end of the Lord: "And it was the third hour, and they crucified him. And the superscription of his accusation was written over, JESUS OF NAZARETH KING OF THE JEWS... And in the sixth hour, there was darkness over the whole land until the ninth hour."

At the ninth hour, Jesus cried with a loud voice, saying, "Eloi, Eloi, lama sabachthani?" Which is interpreted as "My God, My God, why hast thou forsaken me?" One would conclude that the Father would be around to see Jesus expunge himself from the body, which was manufactured with great technology.

John 19:33–34 states, "But when they came to Jesus, and saw that he was dead already, they brake not his legs: But one of the soldiers with a spear pierced his side, and forthwith came there out blood and water."

The Lord Jesus Christ thus completed the atoning sacrifice as soon as his blood was let unto mother earth. The sin of Adam and the curse thereof had been compensated for. On the third day, the blessing affixed to this unusual sacrifice would mature. And, as the songwriter says, "The blessing would go as far as the curse was found."

The apostle Matthew wrote, in Matthew 27:52–54, "And the graves were opened; and many bodies of the saints which slept arose, And came out of the graves after his resurrection and went into the city and appeared unto many. Now when the centurion and they that were with him, watching Jesus, saw the earthquake, and those things that were done, they feared greatly, saying, truly this was the Son of God."

A manifestation of the crucifixion and death of Jesus Christ was witnessed also among the Nephites in the Promised Land in America.

AD 34

Nephi recorded the following in *The Book of Mormon*, 3 Nephi 8:3: "And the people began to look with great earnestness for the sign which had been given by the prophet Samuel, the Lamanite, yea, for the time that there should be darkness for the space of three days over the face of the whole land."

3 Nephi 8:8 states, "And the city of Zarahemla did take fire." Tempests, earthquakes, fires, whirlwinds, and physical upheavals attest to the crucifixion of Christ. Many people were destroyed, darkness covered the land for three days, and those who remained bemoaned their fate.

The records of the Nephites indicate in 3 Nephi 9 that in the darkness, the voice of Christ proclaimed the destruction of many people and cities for their wickedness. He also proclaimed his divinity, announced that the law of Moses was fulfilled, and invited men to come unto him and be saved. He said also unto them in 3 Nephi 9:18–20, I am the light and the life of the world. I am the Alpha and the Omega, the beginning and the end. And ye shall offer up unto me no more the shedding of blood; yea, your sacrifices and burnt offerings shall be done away, for I will accept none of your sacrifices and burnt offerings. And ye shall offer for a sacrifice unto me a broken heart and a contrite spirit. And whoso cometh unto me with a broken heart and a contrite spirit, him will I baptize with fire and the Holy Ghost."

From Jerusalem, the apostle Matthew recorded the following in Matthew 28:1–2, 5–6:

> In the end of the Sabbath, as it begun to dawn towards the first day of the week, came Mary Magdalene and the other Mary to see the Sepulcher. And behold, there was a great earth quake; for the angel of the Lord descended from heaven, and came and rolled back the stone from the door and sat on it… And the angel answered and said unto the woman, fear not ye; for I know that ye seek Jesus which was crucified. He is not here; for he is risen as he said, come, and see the place where the Lord laid.

The apostle John also recounted how he observed the events following the sacrifice of Jesus. He wrote that Mary Magdalene came to the apostles. She said that she had seen the Lord, who spoke to her and said, "touch me not; for I am not yet ascended unto my Father; but go to my brethren and say unto them, I ascend unto my Father, and your Father; and unto my God and your God." John reports also that, that same Sunday at evening, when the disciples had shut themselves up for fear of the Jews, Jesus came and stood in their midst and said unto them, "Peace be unto you". The disciple Thomas, then called Didymus but now popularly called Doubting Thomas, was not with them when Jesus came. Thomas would never believe the other disciples when they told him about the visit by Jesus. After eight days, the disciples were again assembled as before, and this time, Doubting Thomas was with them. "Then came Jesus, the doors being shut, and stood in the midst, and said, "Peace be unto you. Then said he unto Thomas, reach tither thy finger, and behold my hands; and reach tither thy hand and thrust it into my side, and be not faithless but believing. And Thomas answered and said unto him, My Lord and My God. Jesus said unto him, Thomas, because thou has seen me, thou hast believed; blessed are they that have not seen, and yet have believed." **John 20:26-28**

In What Direction Is Religion Drifting?

Our teachers of religion must have missed out on certain evident information that they must stress strongly. It is probably because they have limited their knowledge and therefore their teaching to a few ancient instructors. The first three verses of the Gospel of John in the Christian Bible clearly illustrate that Jesus Christ was referred to as the Word. He was also in the beginning with God.[1] Actually, nothing would have been done without him.

As a pre-mortal spirit being, he performed many functions attributed to the Father. He was the God who led the Jaredites, the Nephites, and the Mulekites, who were later called the people of Zarahemla. Jesus Christ was also known to be the God of Israel. He showed his spirit body to the brother of Jared, and there was no doubt that he was performing the functions of God. It is recorded that Enoch prophesied as commanded by the Lord Jesus Christ. (See Moses 7:2,7 in the Pearl of Great Price.)

During our time, which is known to be the dispensation of the fullness of time, Jesus Christ gave the prophet Joseph Smith the power to lay the foundation of the ultimate church. He was to bring the church out of obscurity and out of darkness. He was told that this was going to be the only true and living church upon the face of the whole earth.

All Christians had been taught that Jesus Christ was the second member of the Godhead. We believe also that the Holy Spirit is the third member and that the Holy Spirit does not have a tabernacle. He is thus the messenger who is able to fuse with the body of the human being and deposit indelible information. This privilege of the Holy Spirit is given only to worthy people. Such people are not forgiven if they should abuse such a privilege. We are thus made to believe that murder and sin against the Holy Spirit are forgiven neither on earth nor in heaven, at the court of Jesus Christ after the resurrection of the dead.

As preachers of the various religions, we are trying to lead people to our God. Sometimes it is evident that the word "God" does not refer to one being. In ancient times, the sun worshippers of the various nations had different names for the sun god according to their various languages.[1] In our current dispensation also, different languages have called God differently, but they refer to the same being. In Ghana and elsewhere, Islam says Allah is the same being that the Christians call God. The Christians and Islamists agree that they are serving the same God according to their chosen practices, and there is harmony.

Of late, however, one wonders if all who profess Jesus Christ are indeed worshipping one Jesus Christ, or if there are types of Jesus Christ. What about Islam? If indeed there is only one Godhead for all religions, then we must be sure where we stand. Evidently, opposing factions, such as Jesus Christ and Satan, will never belong together. It appears, though, that the winner takes all. The doubting Thomas must confirm where he stands, for very soon there will be no more need to cry again for people to repent.

CHAPTER 8

THE RESURRECTION OF THE DEAD

The resurrection of the dead is the ultimate blessing. It is the blessing affixed to the atoning sacrifice undertaken by the Saviour of all mankind, the Lord Jesus Christ. With the fall of Adam in the garden of Eden, he was to die in answer to his disobedience to the law of God in the garden. An immediate death of Adam would have curtailed God's desire to bring to pass the immortality and eternal life of man. In the making of Adam, the spirit Son of God, into the living soul, God had taken an initial mighty action. The action established God's plan for the spirit man, Adam, who had metamorphosed into a living soul to be immortal and to have eternal life.

God thus immediately deferred death, the punishment affixed to the law in the garden of Eden. God then brought into play an alternative plan. The plan was to ensure that man arrived at the planned final destination of immortality and eternal life. This intervention was a stopgap that would allow man to spend time in a probationary period. It was to prevent the failure of the plan, which would have been the case if the man Adam had died immediately. The probationary period made time available for the teaching of Adam to learn to obey God.

In his righteousness and justice, God would not nullify the death penalty that Adam had earned. The death penalty was only suspended. Justice of the law requires that an offender is given punishment commensurate with a crime. God deemed it necessary to make a sacrifice. The sacrifice would serve as propitiation to satisfy justice of the law. After the sacrifice, the sacrificial Lamb of God would have restoration in full of the body and life. The body was lost to the spirit man during the disembodiment of the spirit, which is death. The death of the sacrificial lamb would be painful and humiliating, and it was to be visited upon a sinless individual. That individual would be granted special blessing to benefit mankind, the posterity of the disobedient man Adam. In death, the living soul would be disembodied and the spirit of the Sacrificial Lamb would lose life and body. Soon thereafter, the body and life would be restored. The process would bring immunity to the resurrected soul, which would then know no more death. Restoring man's body so he obtains immortality and eternal life following the first death is what is known as the resurrection of the dead.

In the resurrection, the original body is restored completely without any loss of integrity or any part of the body. The man would appear with the same image and likeness he had during the probation. There is no difference between man

- following his creation in the garden of Eden;
- following the fall, when he was in the probationary period before the first death;
- following the resurrection, before he goes to be judged; or
- after the judgement, when he will continue in eternity.

The descendants of the man Adam would enjoy these blessings.

METAMORPHOSIS OF MAN

The word "metamorphosis" means "gradual change through a series of developmental forms and behaviour to a final definitive form of life". This happens when an egg and sperm fuse into one zygote, which divides into a large number of cells. For up to eight weeks, the developing human being is an embryo. From that time until birth at nine months, the developing human is called a foetus. The foetus starts out having miniature human features. Finally, a fully formed human grows until it is born into a baby, which grows into an adult.

Following man through the metamorphosis, we begin with him as the spirit child of God in heaven, who cannot be discerned by our natural eyes. The material of the spirit is very refined. The book of Hosea says, "Ye are the sons of the living God" (1:10). Also, Jesus said; "...for as the Father hath life in Himself; so hath He given to the son to have life in himself" (John 5:26). The apostle Paul wrote to the Hebrews that we give reverence to the fathers of our flesh on earth. He suggested also that it would be better for us to be submissive, or be in subjugation, to the Father of spirits and live. (See Hebrews 12:9.)

The man in heaven is a spirit, and this spirit man needs to be embodied to have a fullness of joy. (See Doctrine and Covenants 93:33.) Thus, God gave a body to the man, transforming him into a soul that was without life. He then gave him the breath of life, which made him a living soul. Man is made in the likeness and image of God. (See Genesis 1:26.) This completes the metamorphosis of man from the spirit through the soul and finally to the living soul. Sometimes the word "soul" is used to mean something other than the spirit and the body together without the breath of life. "…for man is spirit. The elements are eternal, and spirit and elements inseparably connected, receive the fullness of joy. And when separated, man cannot receive the fullness of joy. The elements are the tabernacle of God" (Doctrine and Covenants 93:33–35).

We now follow the metamorphosis of man, who, being a living soul, falls into probation in mortality following the disobedience in the garden of Eden. Death has been deferred, but the man has lost favour with God. He is now subject to death. The death penalty is executed, and in the process the man suffers disembodiment. He is again only a spirit, just as he was in heaven in the first estate of man. But now he is a dishonoured spirit and is ostracized from the presence of God. The blessings affixed to the atoning sacrifice of Jesus Christ allow man to be resurrected into a living soul for a second time. The man is thus restored into the image and likeness he had when the Father in heaven first created him. The resurrection restores the man perfectly. The prophet Alma teaches the following in *The Book of Mormon*:

> The resurrection brings about the restoration of those things spoken by the prophets. (Alma 40:21–22)

> All things shall be restored to proper order. (Alma 41:4)

> Do not suppose ye shall be restored from sin to happiness. **Alma 41:10**

> Meaning of restoration is to bring back evil for evil, and good for good. Alma (41:12–13)

Because of the resurrection, men are restored to God's presence. (Alma 42:23)

If man has desired evil, evil shall be done unto him, according to the restoration of God. (Alma 42:27–28)

Thereafter the resurrected man is judged and assigned a permanent place in hell or in heaven. All the foregoing references mean that we shall appear before the judgement seat of God as we now are in mortal life.

The scriptures teach us that Jesus Christ was the sacrificial Lamb of God. There is evidence also that on the third day following his death in the circumstances described, he was resurrected. A number of people who had died before him were seen walking in the streets. Matthew 27:52 (3 Nephi 23:9) states that graves were opened and many bodies arose. Jesus Christ testified in Luke 24:39, "…spirit hath no flesh and bones as ye see me have."

A resurrected being has a body of flesh and bones without blood. This is as opposed to those who are brought back to life, being restored to mortality with blood (See *Bible Dictionary*, p. 761).

THE RESURRECTED JESUS CHRIST

Jesus was seen by people who knew him in mortality. Jesus was first seen by Mary on the morning of the resurrection. (See Mark 16:9). Jesus was seen the same first Sunday by the ten apostles when Thomas was not with them. (See Luke 24:30, 36–40). Jesus was seen on the second Sunday, when Thomas was with the rest of the apostles. "Because thou hast seen me thou hast believed" (John 20:29). Jesus stood by the seashore. (See John 21:4). The third time that Jesus showed himself (see John 21:14), Paul saw him, and he was saying unto Paul, "... make haste" (Acts 22:18). He was seen above 500 brethren. (See 1 Corinthians 15:6). "Last of all he was seen of me" (1 Corinthians 15:8).

On the fortieth day before he ascended, he was with the eleven apostles. "And he led them out as far as Bethany, and he lifted up his hands, and blessed them. And it came to pass, while he blessed them, he was parted from them, and carried up into heaven" (Luke 24:50–51).

The reality of the resurrection is that the resurrected Lord was, in every way, the same as he was in mortality when he was with the disciples.

At the age of about thirty-two years, Jesus taught that he was the good shepherd of Israel. In John 10:16, He volunteered very significant information. He said, "And other sheep I have, which are not of this fold; them also I must bring, and they shall hear my voice; and there shall be one-fold, and one shepherd."

There is evidence in *The Book of Mormon* that after the resurrection the Lord appeared to the Nephites in America. (See 3 Nephi 15:11–24). This account is dated AD 34. If the Lord was killed in April AD 34, then he must have appeared to the Nephites within the year following the resurrection. In 3 Nephi 9 in *The Book of Mormon*, the record of the fulfilment of the death of Jesus Christ as prophesied by Samuel the Lamanite is dated AD 34. This period could only be between AD 33 and 34, as the advent of Jesus Christ occurred between AD 33 and 34.

Further accounts of the reality of the resurrected Lord are recorded in 3 Nephi 11. There was a multitude of Nephites gathered together round about the temple which was in the land Bountiful. They were conversing about Jesus Christ, of whom the sign had been given concerning his death. Then they suddenly heard a voice from heaven, which became clearer for their understanding on the third time.

3 Nephi 11:7–12 states that the heavenly voice invited them to behold the beloved son in whom he was pleased, and in whom he had glorified his name. And he invited them to hear him. They did pay attention and saw a man descending out of heaven, and he was clothed in a white robe. He came down and stood in the midst of them, and the eyes of the whole multitude were turned upon him. He spoke unto the people and introduced himself as Jesus Christ, whom the prophets testified shall come into the world. And he stated that he had glorified the Father in taking upon himself the sins of the world in which he had suffered the will of the Father in all things from the beginning. "…the whole multitude fell to the earth; for they remembered that it had been prophesied among them that Christ should show himself unto them after his ascension into heaven" (3 Nephi 11:12).

The Lord asked them to arise and come forth unto him that they might thrust their hands into his side and also that they might feel the prints of the nails in his hands and his feet, that they might know that he was the God of Israel and the God of the whole earth, and that he had been slain for the sins of the whole earth.

This they did do, going forth one by one, until they had all gone forth, and they did see with their own eyes and did feel with their hands, and they did know with surety and did bear record, that it was he, of whom it was written by the prophets, that should come. "And when they had all gone forth and had witnessed for themselves, they cried with one accord, saying: Hosanna! Blessed be the name of the Most High God! And they did fall down at the feet of Jesus and worshipped him" (3 Nephi 11:16–17).

Jesus called Nephi and said unto him, "I give unto thee power that ye shall baptize these people when I am again ascended into heaven" (3 Nephi 11:21).

Jesus thus established his church and taught them just as he did in Israel.

In 3 Nephi 15:12–17, 19–20; Jesus chooses twelve disciples and says,

> Ye are my disciples, who are a remnant of the house of Joseph. And behold, this is the land of your inheritance; and the father hath given it unto you. And not at any time has the Father given me commandments that I should tell it unto your brethren at Jerusalem. Neither at any time has the Father given me commandments that I should tell unto them concerning the other tribes of the house of Israel, whom the Father has sent away out of the land. This much did the Father command me, that I should tell unto them;That other sheep I have which are not of this fold; them also I must bring, and they should hear my voice; and there shall be one-fold and one shepherd.

He said unto them, however, that the Father had commanded him and he was therefore telling them that they were separated from their people in Jerusalem because of their iniquity. That is why those in Israel did not know about the Nephites and the people of Zarahemla who were led out of Jerusalem by Mulek. He was telling them truthfully that the Father had separated other tribes from them because of the iniquity and that that was why they did not know them also.

Overwhelmed by what they experienced, the people said,

"The eye hath never seen, neither hath the ear heard before, so great and marvelous things as we saw and heard Jesus speak unto the Father" (3Nephi 17:16).

Jesus provides bread and wine miraculously and again administers the sacraments unto them. "Now when the multitude had all eaten and drank, behold, they were filled with the Spirit; and they did cry with one voice, and give glory to Jesus, whom they both saw and heard." (3 Nephi 20:9).

It is evident now that Jesus Christ did not need very humble, loving, and concerned people who would not want to shed the blood of any innocent person in Israel. He therefore arranged that such people should not remain in Israel to influence the Jews so that the sacrifice of Jesus Christ, under those wicked circumstances as happened to Jesus Christ, would not happen. If there were such peace-loving people in Jerusalem, Jesus would not have sacrificed because of the influence of those good people. The atoning sacrifice would not have happened, and there would not have been resurrection of the dead. And the atonement would not have been possible, and the curse from the sin of Adam would have remained forever, and man would not go back to God again.

The reality of the resurrection is now undoubted.

The ministry of the apostle Paul, following his encounter with the resurrected Lord, lasted for several decades. He continued his ministry in the presence of the Lord. Paul received encouragement, wisdom, protection, and directives as to what to do and at what time he was to perform his several duties.

Paul recounts his former persecution of the saints as a Pharisee. He testifies of the appearance of Jesus on the Damascus road. The king Agrippa is "almost persuaded" to be a Christian.

Paul reports to King Agrippa In Acts 26 that he saw a light

from heaven brighter than the brightness of the sun shining around him and those who journeyed with him. And when they were all fallen to the earth, he heard a voice speaking to him in the Hebrew language, saying "Saul, Saul, why do you persecute me? It is hard for you to kick against the pricks." Paul then asked, "Who are you, sir, Lord?" And he said he was Jesus Christ, whom Paul was persecuting.

Jesus asked him to stand upon his feet, for he had appeared unto Paul for a purpose—to make him a minister and a witness both to those things that Paul had seen and those things in which Jesus would appear unto him in the future.

Paul would be delivered from the people and the Gentiles, unto whom he was being sent. That would be done to open their eyes, and to turn them from darkness to light and from the power of Satan unto God, that they might receive forgiveness of sins, and inheritance among them that are sanctified by faith in Jesus Christ.

And it came to pass, that, when Paul came again to Jerusalem, while he prayed in the temple, he was in a trance. And he saw Jesus Christ asking him to make haste and get quickly out of Jerusalem, for the people would not receive his testimony concerning Jesus Christ. He asked Paul to depart, for he was sending him far away to the Gentiles. (See Acts 22:17–18, 21.)

The following night, the Lord stood by Paul and asked him to be of good cheer and told him that as Paul had testified of Jesus in Jerusalem, he would also have to bear witness at Rome. (See Acts 23:11.)

All these things illustrate that the resurrected Lord was still at work just as he was in mortality. This shows that the resurrection of the dead restores the man perfectly to what he was in mortality. His pattern teaches that we will be restored to the same image and likeness we have now. Here in mortality, we are able to hide and conceal our wickedness. This is even when we are of the principalities, powers, and the rulers of the darkness of this world, exercising spiritual wickedness against everyone with whom we come into contact. (See Ephesians 6:12). We are warned that the angels are recording all our thoughts, words, and deeds from birth to death. We shall be judged according to those things which are written in the Book of Life.

The apostle Paul was drafted into service soon after the resurrection of the Lord. In our current dispensation, the dispensation of the fullness of time, the prophet Joseph Smith has concluded the message of the atonement. He sealed it with his blood.

The Doctrine and Covenants of the Church of Jesus Christ of Latter-day Saints are revelations received by Joseph Smith. The prophet illustrates the voice of the resurrected Jesus Christ in *The Book of Mormon*, Alma 12:28. A revelation given to the prophet Joseph Smith in April 1829 is recorded in Doctrine and Covenants 6:21: "Behold, I am Jesus Christ, the Son of God. I am the same that came unto my own, and my own received me not. I am the light which shineth in darkness, and the darkness comprehendeth it not."

And again, on March 7, 1831 the prophet Joseph Smith received a revelation from the Lord.

> And then shall the Jews look upon me and say: What are these wounds in thine hands and thy feet? Then shall they know that I am the Lord; for I will say unto them: These wounds are the wounds with which I was wounded in the house of my friends. I am he who was lifted up. I am Jesus that was crucified. I am the Son of God. And

then shall they weep because of their iniquities; then shall they lament because they persecuted their king. And then shall the heathen nations be redeemed, and they that knew no law shall have part in the first resurrection; and it shall be tolerable for them. (Doctrine and Covenants 45:51–54; also see Zachariah 13:6)

This information of the atonement and the resurrection of the dead is available to the whole world. Jesus Christ tells us that he is God not only of Israel but of the whole world. He will judge all the descendants of Adam and of Noah. These include those who have continued to hate him as well as those who have loved him and are familiar with him. May the world take note of this information and work with it for their salvation. This will contribute to glorify the Lord God Almighty, our Father in heaven, and his only Son begotten in the flesh, our Lord and saviour Jesus Christ, the Lamb of God, who atoned for the sins of the whole world.

CHAPTER 9

THE ECCLESIASTIC

G od, who made Adam and planted him in the garden of Eden, gave him guidance by visiting him regularly. God taught Adam how to have dominion over all the other creations and to subdue the earth and everything in it. But Adam received instructions, teachings, and guidance contrary to those of the Lord. He was thus faced with the need to exercise his agency to choose between two offers. Agency brings the responsibility to make informed choices. It enables one not to make wrongful choices. No living human being would choose to die under normal circumstances. If anybody makes any choice that he knows will lead to death, then he must have been convinced that his death would bring positive benefits as in the atonement of Jesus Christ.

We read in Genesis 3:4–6, "And the serpent said unto the woman, ye shall not surely die…" God had earlier spoken to the man in Genesis 2:16, saying, "But of the tree of knowledge of good and evil, thou shall not eat of it; for in the day that thou eatest thereof ye shall surely die." Was the man deceived to make a misguided choice? God said, "Thou shall surely die." And the devil said, "Ye shall not surely die." Adam makes a choice that leads to death. Did he want a choice that would lead him to die? Or did he realize that he had made a misguided wrong choice that was going to lead to death? Was God happy with Adam's choice, or was the devil the winner at the end of the day? It is a different ball game altogether in deceitfulness, as in Genesis 3:4–6. It became necessary for God to resort to an alternative plan to fulfil his desire to bring to pass the immortality and eternal life of man. He brought in the corrective probationary period. He brought in the atonement to bring about the power that would restore the man, for as recorded in Genesis 2:7 and Abraham 5:7, "The spirit man from Heaven had been made a living soul before it became necessary that he should die."

By this misguided action in the garden of Eden, in disobedience to the law of God, Adam fell. He brought death unto all men. In his wisdom and love for the man, God circumvented the immediate death of man. Death was the punishment affixed to the law in the garden of Eden. He instituted the plan of redemption and the salvation of man with a necessary prerequisite probationary period. It gave man a chance to repent. But justice would, at the end of the 70 to 120 years of probation, invoke the suspended death sentence. Man would die. The breath of life would leave the man. The spirit man component of the soul would leave eternally. The body would crumble into dust and back to Mother Earth.

Thus, justice has not been denied its enforcement of the law. It inflicts death, which is the punishment affixed to answer the ends of the broken law in the garden of Eden.

On the other hand, the atonement of the blood of Jesus Christ invokes the power of the resurrection of the dead. Resurrection is affixed to answer the ends of the atonement of the only Son of God begotten in the flesh. The power of the resurrection brings back the dust from Mother Earth, reconstitutes the body, and restores everything perfectly. The departed spirit is brought back, and the spirit and the body are reunited. The body is restored to its own spirit, and the spirit to its own body, never to be divided. The man is thus restored into the presence of God.

Then comes the judgement, which makes a difference between the disobedient and the penitent souls according to their thoughts, words, and deeds during mortal life, the period of probation. At judgement, God the father; Jesus Christ, the sacrificial Lamb of God; and the apostles of the Lord will sit at the court. At this court the Book of Life will be opened. The book will have the record of the thoughts, words, and deeds of man in mortality. These will be the witnesses, as indicated in the Book of Revelation. (See Revelation 20:12–13).

At the judgement seat, it will be evident to all that God is a just God and a merciful God also. Two very great and very important happenings, which are equal and opposite, will happen simultaneously. It will show a difference between the disobedient and the penitent sons and daughters of our God. Justice will not be denied its enforcement of the law, and it will punish. Neither will mercy be denied its role to administer peace and comfort to the embattled soul. The Almighty God sent messages to all his sons and daughters in the world without exception, for Jesus Christ represents the interest of all mankind. A very old man, Simeon of Jerusalem, when he saw the baby Jesus at the temple, said, "Lord, now lettest thou thy servant depart in peace according to thy word. For my eyes have seen thy salvation, which thou hast prepared before the face of all people" (Luke 2:29–30).

Jesus Christ was sent to the world as the antidote for the curse that Adam's action invoked upon all his descendants—the entire human race. The most likely reason why Jesus Christ was sent to the Jews is recorded in 2 Nephi 10:3: "Wherefore, as I said unto you, it must needs be expedient that Christ —

should come among the Jews, among those who are the more wicked parts of the world; and they shall crucify him — for thus it behooveth our God, and there is none other nation on earth that would crucify their God."

Sometimes people have to act wickedly to bring about peace. Retrospectively, a wicked act may later be seen as a kind gesture. By dint of medical history, the doctors in Britain drop the title "Doctor" when they qualify as surgeons and change from Doctor (Dr) to "Mister" (Mr). Before anaesthesia was invented, it was a wicked act to amputate the gangrenous leg of a diabetic patient. The refined medical doctor would not do it. Barbers with their hair dressing shops in the neighbourhood were invited to perform the amputation. The patient was made drunk with alcohol, and the hefty barber gave one blow with the axe. The doctor would then close the wound. Therefore, for every amputation, they would call Mr Barber. With the advent of anaesthesia, the doctor did the surgery of amputation. Now they could call Mr Doctor for the surgery. It happens that I also changed my titles on 11 November 1977 at the Royal College of Surgeons when I qualified as a surgeon. I performed the amputation of the remaining leg of a diabetic. He brought to me a beautiful flying tie. He was very grateful and said, "It was more peaceful this time." Israel was evidently wicked to Jesus Christ. Without that behaviour of apparent wickedness, the atonement would have been impossible. Israel is thus blessed. They only have to accept Jesus as the Christ and they will have no problem.

In ancient times, many simple and ordinary people bore testimony of the peculiar man that Jesus Christ was when they had personal interactions with him. The apostle John recorded the following in John 4:25: "The woman said unto him, I know that the Messiah cometh which is called Christ: when he is come he will tell us all things."

He also states in John 7:31, "And many of the people believed on him, and said, when Christ cometh; will he do more miracles than these which this man hath done?"

At that time, Jesus Christ was about thirty-two years of age (about 1,984 years prior to the year AD 2016).

In the year AD 34, after the resurrection, Jesus Christ testified of himself and said, as recorded in 3 Nephi 9:15–20,

> Behold, I am Jesus Christ the Son of God. I created the heavens and the earth, and all things that in them are. I was with the Father from the beginning. I am in the Father and the Father in me: and in me hath the Father glorified his name. I came unto my own, and my own received me not. And the scriptures concerning me are fulfilled. And as many as have received me, to them have I given to become the sons of God; and even so will I to as many as shall believe on my name, for behold, by me redemption cometh, and in me the law of Moses is fulfilled. I am the light and the life of the world. I am Alpha and Omega, the beginning and the end. And ye shall offer up unto me no more the shedding of blood; yea, your sacrifices and your burnt offerings shall be done away, for I will accept none of your sacrifices and your burnt offerings. And ye shall offer for a sacrifice unto me a broken heart and a contrite spirit. And whoso cometh unto me with a broken heart and a contrite spirit, him will I baptize with fire and with the Holy Ghost.

Just as Judaism still exists and probably still upholds the law of Moses, so also do numerous other religious institutions across the world. These are in addition to the Christian religion. Many of these other religions recognize Jesus Christ as one of the numerous other prophets of God. They do not ascribe any more superiority to the Lord than they do others. Likewise, Nathaniel had to meet Jesus Christ face-to-face before he repented and recognized the Lord. Nathaniel answered and said unto him, "Rabbi, thou art the Son of God; thou art the king of Israel" (John 1:49).

Some of these religious institutions are so obsessively against Jesus Christ that they hate anything Christian. They have, in practise, declared war, which they fight unilaterally and in secret. They have stigmatized themselves as evil. They do not want to be identified with that institution to which they belong. The Book of Mormon prophets refer to these institutions as "Secret Combinations." They do not support just laws, which do not function in secret and in hiding. All are descendants of Adam living on this earth. The ongoing cry for repentance must be heeded by all who count themselves descendants of Adam, and also of Noah, who became the father of all living after the flood. All people living on the earth must know that at the end of this period of probation on the earth, at the end of the allowed life span of 70 to 120 years, man will die. This means that

- the breath of life will be withdrawn,
- the spirit man will depart, and
- the earthen body will crumble into its Mother Earth.

They must know also that the power of the resurrection of the dead, which is affixed to answer the ends of the atonement of the blood of Jesus Christ, will restore all things. It will subdue death, undo everything that death has done, and effect the resurrection of the dead. This means that

- the dust will be gathered and reconstituted into the body with the restoration of all its constituents,
- the spirit will be recalled from being ostracized to be reunited with its body, and
- the soul will be restored to life, no more to be divided.

The first two of these events will generally happen to both the wicked and the good, whether they are for Jesus Christ or against him.

Now the man has been resurrected from the first spiritual death. In that death he was ostracized from before the presence of God. He is now brought back into the presence of God as Adam was before the fall. The atonement of the blood of Jesus Christ has fulfilled its purpose. It has brought man into the presence of God. Now this physically healthy man, who is for all intents and purposes very much like us in the flesh, is ready for judgement at the court of God. The Father; Jesus Christ, the Lamb of God; and the apostles with them will judge all children of men.

The theme of this court is repentance, and judgement takes account only of mortal life. Jesus Christ, who enjoyed the right of the firstborn Son in heaven, now has greater honour and glory bestowed upon him. This is because he offered himself to be the sacrifice for sin in the plan for the redemption and salvation of every man. He is honoured with this court. Here the atonement and the resurrection of the dead have already been fulfilled. Man is again in the presence of God. According to Revelation 20:12–13, the file for this court will be the Book of Life. In there is written everything that man did in mortality. The wrongs that he thought, said, or performed, for which he might have sincerely repented and asked for pardon, will be closely examined at the court. It must be understood, however, that the sin against the Holy Ghost and murder are not forgiven here in this world or in the world to come.

WHY I AM HARPING ABOUT THE ATONEMENT

The ancient prophet Hosea taught that forgetting the law of God, which makes us lack knowledge, amounts to rejecting knowledge. God said then that people are destroyed because they reject knowledge. In other words, when we reject his laws, he will also reject us and we shall be destroyed. Hosea died about 736 BC, according to the *Bible Dictionary*.

Jesus Christ started his teachings about AD 30, and his theme was that people must repent because the kingdom of God was at hand. That was about 2,750 years ago this year (2018). Jesus Christ hammered on his message that the forgiveness of our sins against God would happen if we would repent before we shut our eyes in death. This is the message given by Jesus Christ, which formed the basis of his teachings. He preached that if man repented from his disobedience to the law of God before he died, then he could most likely be free from punishment following death and the judgement which will follow the resurrection of the dead.

Before the demise of Moses, God had given man several laws. Each of these laws has a prescribed punishment attached to it. The most severe punishment that could come to all men would ostracize them permanently from God following death, which is the result of Adam's transgression. Fortunately for man, God, by the atoning sacrifice of Jesus Christ, has brought man into his presence again. Blessings from the atoning sacrifice invoke the power of resurrection of the dead, which brings man back to life the second time—and permanently.

Unfortunately, the lifestyle of man in our days illustrates

that man has deliberately decided to disobey God; he does many things that he knows will infuriate God. Man is calling the bluff and saying, as it were, "Get me if you can." God, on the other hand, has specified certain behaviours which he says are abominable and that man must abstain from. Following are a few of the actions that are abominable unto God. Some of these laws were forerunners of the atonement, wherein an unblemished, sinless individual—mostly lambs but also goats and cattle—were used as propitiation between estranged parties. These were emphasized greatly, leading to millions of such sacrifices by the Israelites. As an aside to these blood sacrifices and burnt offerings, it was forbidden to eat blood and fat. These blood sacrifices were discontinued upon the resurrection of Jesus Christ.

There were other laws which had no bearing on the atonement. Those were about abominable behaviours which God detested. The books of Moses are referred to as the Law, but the third book, Leviticus, is the one which spells out most of the laws with prescribed punishments attached. Here are a few examples: "A man should not lie with another man as with a woman; this is abomination to God. Neither shall a man lie with any beast to defile himself therewith: Neither shall any woman stand before a beast to lie down thereto: This is confusion" (Leviticus 18:22–23).

God says it is because the nations the Israelites encountered during the Exodus were similarly defiled that he cast them out before the Israelites. God warned the Israelites not to commit these abominations. He warned the Israelites that any of them who committed any of these abominations would be cut out from off their people. These were and still are simple and pure abominations that God detests. These abominations defiled the land.

But what do we read in the journals these days? Two men presented themselves at a church and asked to be married. The priest naturally refused the request. He incurred the fury of a recently enacted law that seeks to force the priest against God, whom he represents. A sheep had a baby with a human head and four legs. These stories were reported in AD 2018, thanks to rapid advancements in telecommunications, which has reduced the whole world to a small community of humans and animals. God does not take it kindly when man drags him into shame by using his body inappropriately, for God made man in his own image and likeness.

The foregoing are examples of serious offences against God. He evidently hates such offences. He appears to have relinquished his judgement seat to the "Crown Prince", the Lord Jesus Christ, who is waiting cautiously for the days of judgement, which are evidently not far from hence. He knows that each person will have his Book of Life, wherein is a true record of his life activities. I believe that each one of us, on arrival at the judgement seat, will be reminded that we were warned to repent before arriving at the judgement seat. Unfortunately, some of us have already opted for the weeping and gnashing of the teeth and the appropriate degree of a kingdom. Their choices will be available without fail. We must not deceive ourselves, for the unrighteous will not resurrect into righteousness. I am thus taking advantage again to do the crying for our Lord Jesus Christ: Repent! Repent, for the kingdom of God is at hand!

CONCLUSION

THE ATONEMENT BECAME NECESSARY

I f God the Father had not planned to establish the immortality and eternal life of the Spirit in heaven, there would have been no thought of disembodying the living soul in the process of death. Thus there would have been no atonement necessary.

On the other hand, if the evil one had not enticed Adam to disobey God the Father, there would also have been no punishment unto death by the process of disembodiment of the living soul. The restoration would not have been necessary.

But once upon a time, it became needful to kill the sinless Lord, Jesus Christ, as the sacrificial Lamb of God. Justice and grace had to be reconciled to make available the blessing that would go as far as the curse of Adam would be found.

Just as God was happy at the end of each day of the creation, so also must he have rejoiced after he had succeeded to join the spirit of man inseparably with the elements into the living soul. God has said, "This is my work and my glory to bring to pass the immortality and eternal life of man" (Moses 1:39). It's no wonder that he instituted and established the atonement and the resurrection of the dead. God was capable of doing whatever came to his mind. God has said also, "There is nothing that the Lord thy God shall take in his heart to do but what he will do it" (Abraham 3:17).

The world is reminded that a majority of the people who saw and heard Jesus Christ did not have the knowledge and understanding of the atonement as we do now, having read the foregoing messages. If indeed 1,000 years on Earth make one day in the abode of God, then the six working days when time is relevant for toiling have ended. The end of the dispensation of the fullness of time is at hand, as we are 6,000 years from the day of Adam. The beginning of the seventh day of the sabbatical rest of the millennium is soon to be ushered in. Time has run out for those who are still looking for another messiah to come.

For these several thousands of years here on Earth, the cry has been "Repent, for the kingdom of God is at hand!" Jesus Christ is still beckoning to all living souls. There is no other man who lived on the earth whose history is known from the creation of the earth by God until now. The only other spirit child of God whose history is known from the war in heaven is Satan. He never had a body, and he will never have one of his own. He remains a spirit and is ostracized from before the presence of God the Father. Spiritually he is dead eternally, for he cannot ever be in the presence of the Almighty God the Father. There is therefore no other messiah to come besides the only Son of God begotten in the flesh: he who has atoned for the sin of the world with his blood—Jesus the Christ.

Beloved worldly people, this is most probably the last cry in great distress, saying, "Repent! Repent, for indeed the kingdom of God is at hand!" The atonement brings the responsibility to man to be meek and righteous in order to have and enjoy the full benefits of the blessings emanating from the atonement of our Lord Jesus Christ.

Give glory to God. All that we do must be done with an eye single to the glory of God.

Have faith in the Lord Jesus Christ, for he is merciful and true, and he brings us into the presence of God. Jesus Christ is still beckoning to all living souls. He says, "Be not faithless, but believing. For blessed are they that have not seen, and yet have believed" (John 20:29). Amen.

"There is nothing that the Lord thy God shall take in his heart to do but what he will do it." Abraham 3:17

APPENDIX 1

THE PLAGUES OF "LET MY PEOPLE GO" IN EGYPT

- Exodus 7:17   Waters turned to blood
- Exodus 8:2   All borders smitten with frogs
- Exodus 8:16   Dust turned to become lice
- Exodus 8:21   Swarm of flies
- Exodus 9:3   Cattle suffer grievous murrain
- Exodus 9:9   Boils breaking forth with blisters and pustules
- Exodus 9:18   Very grievous hailstorm
- Exodus 10:4   Locusts
- Exodus 10:22   Thick darkness in Egypt
- Exodus 11:5   The firstborn in Egypt made to die
- Exodus 12:29   Smiting by the Lord of all the firstborn in the land of Egypt, from the firstborn of Pharaoh that sat on his throne unto the firstborn of the captive that was in the dungeon, and all the firstborn of cattle

APPENDIX 2

THE AKANS AND AKAN INVOLVEMENT IN LANDS OF EXCITING HISTORY

Abraham (called Abram in early life) was born in the ancient city of Ur in the land of Chaldea in the year 1996 BC. The family relocated to Haran in Mesopotamia (now Syria), which Abraham called his country.

From Haran, Abraham moved to live in Damascus, where he picked for a manservant Eliezer, who became his chief servant. From there he went to the land of Canaan and lived in Hebron. This is where he settled on his return from Egypt. This finally became their home in a country where they were strangers. God promised to give the land to him that is his posterity, after 400 years of apparent slavery.

On his return from Egypt with his wife, Sarah, Abraham was very rich. His nephew Lot was also rich. For the purpose of their menservants not fighting over feeding grounds for their animals, they parted. Lot chose the plains of Jordan—the south eastern part of the land, where the cities of Sodom and Gomorrah were. Abraham had the land of Canaan and moved his tent to Hebron in the plains of Mamre. God promised him there to give to him the land of Canaan, which did not include the southern parts and the land of Seir. (See Genesis 13:14–15, 18.)

While there, Lot was taken prisoner of war by a group of four kings and their armies who came from the land of Mesopotamia. The king of Shinar was included. Shinar's king was Nimrod, and he built the tower of Babel. Abraham was informed, and with 300 men from his house, he pursued these armies to Damascus and brought back all the people and everything that was taken. On his return, he was met by Melchizedek from the city of Jebusites called Jebus/Salem. That was when Abraham paid tithes of all his possession to Melchizedek, who was the king over the Jebusites.

In the course of time, Sarah, in her old age, had Isaac for Abraham. Isaac also had twins, Esau and Jacob. Esau (Edom) married two Canaanite wives. One was a Hittite, and the other was Hivite. His third wife was a daughter of Ishmael, Abraham's son.

Esau lived in the land of Canaan at Hebron and became prosperous. Jacob, on the other hand, went back to Haran to marry from his ancestral home. He was also blessed with twelve sons; Diana is the only daughter named. Meanwhile, Hivite, the sixth son of Canaan, had a son named Hori (a controversial name with varied spellings), whose son Seir had seven sons. The first of Seir's sons was Lotan, whose first son was also called Hori. Seir's sixth son, Ezar also had three sons, and the third of these sons was called AKAN.

These people now called Horites settled in the mountainous area known as Mount Seir or the land of Seir. This was in a mountainous ridge that ran south of the Dead Sea through the land that was originally inhabited by the Horites. (See Genesis 14:6). Seir the Horite and his sons inhabited Mount Seir when Esau (Edom) got there. The sons of Seir who were the dukes of the Horites were Lotan, Shobal, and Zibeon, and Anah, Dishon, Ezar, and Dishan. The grandfather, Hori, father of Seir, is believed to have dwelt in some of the several caves of Mount Seir on the east side. When Lot left Sodom through Zoar when God destroyed the place, he left from the west to the east with his two daughters, who had one son each with their father. They were Moab and Ammon, who also settled on the east side of the Salt Sea.

Now Esau, observing the wealth of his brother Jacob when he returned from Haran with greater wealth, moved to the lowlands of Mount Seir, which then became known as Edom after Esau (Edom). On the arrival of Jacob from Haran, Esau came from Seir to meet him. He then went back to Seir, and Jacob went his way to Succoth and build a house there, and he called the name of the place El-elohe-Israel (meaning "God is the God of Israel").

Now the Akan had not been lost in this hurly-burly of striving for a dwelling place that would be convenient for life's activities and historical scenes. The Akans migrated from the north, from the land of Seir, about AD 500 through Egypt. They arrived in Nubia or East Sudan, where pressure exerted by the Axumite Kingdom of Ethiopia shattered Nubia, and the Akans moved west. They moved from the Sahara Desert and Sahel region of Africa around AD 1100. The empire of Ghana was founded in AD 750 and lasted until AD 1200 (a period of 450 years).

The Akans moved, as Islam was introduced in Western Sudan and the Muslims were forcing their religion on the Akans. They left for Kong, which is now Cote d'Ivoire. They moved from Kong to Wam and Dormaa, both of which are in present-day Brong Ahafo. They moved because they were not used to forest life, and they went to savannah land. From

Dormaa they moved to Twifo Hemang, which is north west of Cape Coast. This move was for commercial reasons.

Bonoman or Brong Ahafo was established in the twelfth century (AD 1200–1299). A gold boom between the twelfth and thirteenth centuries brought wealth to many Akans. They migrated for gold and cash crops and business. Finally, the Asante Empire (1700 to 1900) came into existence.

In Summary

Migration from the land of Seir (named Edom for Esau's descendants) in the north, through Egypt, is concluded. Peoples and nations and their inheritance on the earth are generally concluded. Such mass movement as that seen with Israel and also with the Akans is not possible any longer.

The current total population of Akans, 20 million, is found in Ghana and Cote d'Ivoire. Of these, 11, 500, 000 are in Ghana, and 8, 500, 000 in Cote d'Ivoire. These are mainly Twi, Fante, and Bono. There are several subgroups, however, as follows:

Asante	Agona
Akyem	Wassa
Akuapem	Anomabo
Fante	Gomoa
Bono	Abura
Kwahu	

These are the Akans in Ghana.

APPENDIX 3

ABRAHAM'S HEAVENLY VISION

And God saw these sons that they were good, and he stood in the midst of them, and he said: These I will make my rulers; for he stood among those that were spirits, and he saw that they were good; and he said unto me: Abraham, thou art one of them; thou wast chosen before thou wast born. (Abraham 3:23)

APPENDIX 4

DUST THOU ART

The periodic table of elements which constitute the earth (otherwise called variously as the soil, or dust) shows 118 elements that constitute the earth. These are either metal or non-metal, with varying consistencies and strengths, being solid, liquid, or gas at room temperature, with functions peculiar to each element.

With this array of possibilities for the use of these elements, God can do anything that comes to his heart, as he told Abraham. (See Abraham 3:7.) The elements are the building blocks for God. During intrauterine existence and after birth, man is fed with these elements to build the body. So it is also with plants.

A seed germinates by using these elements. A seedling continues to enlarge and to grow using these same elements, and so a little seed grows into a mighty tree and lives for a long time. The scriptures tell us that in the millennium, a child will grow to the age of a tree (Doctrine and Covenants 101:29–31.) Both the tree and the man continue to exist by using the elements in the dust for nourishment.

When both of them, the man and the plant, die, they disintegrate and go back home as elements of the dust and soil of the earth, from which they were taken to form and maintain the man and the plant. Mother Earth receives both of them happily. Man must know that, being a spirit from heaven, he has been given a house by God's crafty handiwork that makes the man compatible with the planet earth.

Just as the wood of the tree differs remarkably from the flesh of the man and other animals, so also are both the plants and the animals, including man, different from the dust of the earth; all of them are of the same primary material—the element that constitutes the dust of the earth, which is the soil.

So then, when God said, "dust thou art," he had hit the nail on the head. Man must therefore examine his ways with regard to what God wants man to do in order to qualify to enter the rest provided by God. Man must desist from incurring the displeasure of God any longer to prevent any further utterances of "Dust thou art and unto dust shalt thou return."

APPENDIX 5

THE POWER TO LAY DOWN HIS LIFE AND TAKE IT UP AGAIN

J esus had the power to lay down his life, and he had the power to take it again. (See Matthew 27:50; John 10:17–18; 19:33–34).

Jesus had said that nobody takes his life and that he had the power to lay it down and the power to take it again. His crucifixion occurred late in the afternoon on Friday. The Sabbath starts at 6.00 p.m. on Friday, and crucified bodies must be taken down, dead, before removal for burial before 6.00 p.m.

The crucifiers came back to break the legs and killed all who were not dead. Before they got to Jesus Christ, he had already given up the ghost. He did not have to be killed. Unknown to the executioners, the blood of Jesus Christ was to flow down to the ground. He had been pierced on the left side of the chest as he was still on the cross. The spear hit the skin and entered the body, going through the stomach and its watery sludge and then into the heart. And so there was a gush of water first, followed by blood.

The atonement was completed as soon as the blood hit the ground. The process of the atonement had started with his arrest on Thursday night. He was insulted and assaulted before his trial and beaten mercilessly. He was finally crucified on Friday, and he was dead before the start of the Sabbath.

> And when Jesus had cried with a loud voice, he said, Father, into thy hands I commend my spirit: and having said thus, he gave up the ghost. (Luke 23:46)

> Therefore, doth my Father love me, because I lay down my life, that I might take it again. No man taketh it from me, but I lay it down myself. I have power to lay it down, and I have power to take it again. This commandment have I received of my Father. (John 10:17–18)

> But when they came to Jesus and saw that he was dead already, they brake not his legs. But one of the soldiers with the spear pierced his side, and forthwith came there out blood and water. (John 19:33–34)

APPENDIX 6

SIMILITUDE OF SACRIFICES

With the completion of the plan and organization of the atonement, Adam must have been one of the earliest to receive the message that was sent abroad. He went ahead to offer the firstlings of his flock as a sacrifice unto God. An angel explained to Adam that the sacrifice he was performing with a lamb was "a similitude of the sacrifice of the Only Begotten of the Father, which is full of grace and truth." **Moses 5:7**

The time of this encounter with the angel is not known, but it would be more than 3,000 years BC. The future event with Jesus Christ, the Lamb of God, was sure to happen in its due time, so the angel was at liberty to teach Adam.

The times of Abraham and Jesus Christ were far in the future. Abraham was asked to sacrifice not an unblemished lamb but his only begotten son, for Isaac was, properly, the only begotten son in marriage. At the moment Abraham was ready to sacrifice his son Isaac, the angel could have properly said of the occasion, "This thing is a similitude of the sacrifice of the Only Begotten of the Father, which is full of grace and truth."

Abraham must have had severe heart pain, but he would not deny the request from God to sacrifice Isaac. Similarly, God would not annul the law of the garden of Eden, because he needed Adam to play a very important, nearly indispensable, role in his "work and his glory to bring to pass the immortality and eternal life of man."

Abraham's need to sacrifice Isaac to God was a similitude to God's need to sacrifice Jesus Christ. How could Abraham have refused God's request? Similarly, God himself had the need to sacrifice his sinless, unblemished, and Only Son Begotten in the flesh, Jesus Christ. This is because God had the need to propitiate for Adam's infringement of the law of the garden of Eden to forestall failure of his plan for the immortality and eternal life of man. God says of the plan, "This is my work and my glory…"

There is indeed a similarity for need for the two sacrifices. In each case, it was not a need for direct personal gain, but it was urgent. Similar to the request for Abraham's sacrifice are the millions of sacrifices with lambs which were symbolic precedence of the atoning sacrifice with the Lamb of God, which was to end sacrifice and bloodshed. See appendix 11, "The Last Sacrifice: The Lamb of God".

APPENDIX 7

THE FATHER AND THE SON

In 3 Nephi 1:14, Jesus Christ himself explains why he refers to himself as both the Father and the Son. He says in 3Nephi 1:14, "…The will both of the Father and the Son-of the Father because of me, and of the Son because of my flesh"

At this time, the spirit was still in heaven, and the body (the flesh) was labouring on earth with Mary, his mother. This account illustrates further the creation of the living man from his components. First, the Spirit man in heaven needs to be housed. Secondly, the building materials are the elements on the earth, which he uses to mould and form the body/ house for the spirit man. The spirit, then with the Father in heaven, spoke to Nephi to announce that he was coming into the house that had been formed and kneaded into the flesh with correct proportions of compatible elements, which are the natural constituents of the soil of the earth. At birth, the spirit takes possession of the body.

Every obstetrician and every midwife who delivers babies must have observed that the first breath of life is very crucial in the successful conclusion of the metamorphosis of the spirit man from heaven through the soul, which is a combination of spirit and body, finally resulting in, with the addition of the breath of life, the living soul at birth. The living soul, therefore, is a triple combination of body, spirit, and breath of life.

APPENDIX 8

CUSTOM OF THE LAW OF MOSES (LAW OF PURIFICATION)

And the LORD spake unto the children of Israel saying speak unto the children of Israel saying, if a woman have conceived seed, and born a male child: then she shall be unclean seven days; according to the days of separation for her infirmity shall she be unclean. And in the eighth day the flesh of his foreskin shall be circumcised. And she shall then continue in the blood of her purifying three and thirty days; she shall touch no hallowed thing, nor come into the sanctuary, until the days of her purifying being fulfilled. (Leviticus 12:1–4)

And when the days of her purifying are fulfilled, for a son, or for a daughter, she shall bring a lamb of the first year for a burned offering, and a young pigeon, or turtledove, for a sin offering, into the door of the tabernacle of the congregation, unto the priest: Who shall offer it before the LORD and make atonement for her; and she shall be cleansed from the issue of her blood. This is the law for her that have born a male or female. And if she be not able to bring a lamb, then she shall bring two turtledoves or two young pigeons: the one of the burnt offering; and the other for a sin offering; and the priest shall make atonement for her, and she shall be cleaned. (Leviticus 12:6–8)

APPENDIX 9

MELCHIZEDEK

The first and the only time recorded in the Bible that Abraham met Melchizedek was in the land of the Jebusite. That was when the king of Sodom went to meet Abraham after his return from the slaughter of Chedorlaomer and the kings that were with him. "And Melchizedek King of Salem brought forth bread and wine; and he was the priest of the most high God... And (Melchizedek) blessed Abraham, and said, Blessed be Abram of the most high God, possessor of heaven and earth. And blessed be the most high God, which hath delivered thine enemies into thine hands. And he (Abram) gave him tithes of all" (Genesis 14: 18–20).

In addition to the Bible presentation, further information was found by the prophet Joseph Smith, who translated the Holy Bible from the ancient languages. The prophet of our time added a rather important omission to this chapter of the scriptures.

> And Melchizedek lifted up his voice and blessed Abram. Now Melchizedek was a man of faith, who wrought righteousness; and when a child he feared God, and stopped the mouths of lions, and quenched the violence of fire. And thus, having been approved of God, he was ordained a high priest after the order

of the covenant which God made with Enoch. It being after the order of the Son of God; which order comes not by man nor the will of man; neither by father or mother; neither by beginning of days nor end of years; but of God; And it was delivered unto men by the calling of his own voice, according to his own will, unto as many as believed on his name. For God having sworn unto Enoch and unto his seed with an oath, by himself; and everyone being ordained after this order and calling should have power, by faith, to break mountains, to divide the sea, to dry up waters, to turn them out of their course; To put at defiance the armies of nations, to divide the earth, to break every band, to stand in the presence of God; to do all things according to his will, according to his command, subdue principalities and powers; and this by the will of the Son of God which was from before the foundation of the world. And men having this faith, coming up unto this order of God, were translated and taken up into heaven. (Note similitude: Enoch, Melchizedek, Moses, Elijah. Is there anything common about these people?) And now, Melchizedek was a priest of this order; therefore, he obtained peace in Salem, and was called the Prince of Peace, And his people wrought righteousness, and obtained heaven, and sought for the city of Enoch which God had before taken, separating it from the earth, having reserved it unto the latter days, or the end of the world; And had said, and sworn with an oath, that the heavens and the earth should come together; and the Son of God should be tried as by fire. And this Melchizedek, having thus established righteousness, was called the King of heaven by his people, or, in other words, the King of peace. And he lifted up his voice, and blessed Abram, being the high priest, and the keeper of the storehouse of God; Him whom God had appointed to receive tithes for the poor. Wherefore, Abram paid unto him tithes of all that he had, of all the riches which he possessed, which God had given him more than that which he had need. And it came to pass, that God blessed Abram, and gave unto him riches, and honour, and lands for an everlasting possession; according to the covenant which he had made, and according to the blessing wherewith Melchizedek had blessed him. (Genesis 14:25–40)

This additional account of Melchizedek from the prophet Joseph Smith's translation of the Bible (JST) makes the account more meaningful. Additionally, it is known from Google social media research that the name Melchizedek is an old Canaanite name.

Evidently the Hebrew people, having been very impressed by the institution of Melchizedek, adopted his expression when he blessed Abram, their spiritual leader. They would then say that the god whom Melchizedek served as priest was El Elyon, which translates as "the Most High God" or God Most High". This expression in the blessing of Abram (i.e., the God Most High) became a favourite expression of the Hebrews. Obviously that was their first time hearing it. The language of the Canaanite Jebusites: king of Salem, priest of El Elyon (i.e., Priest of God Most High). **Genesis 14:18-20, 22.** Jacob's house in Succoth was called El-elohe-Israel.

APPENDIX 10

SATAN'S MODUS OPERANDI

There are a number of statements attributed to great persons in ancient times. This brings to mind the teaching by Our Lord Jesus Christ using the parable of the sower, the wheat, and the tares, which calls us to be aware of similar situations in our lives. Following is what the Master Teacher says in Matthew 13:24–28, 38–39.

> Another parable put he forth unto them saying. The kingdom of heaven is likened unto a man which sowest good seeds in his field: But while men slept, his enemy came and sowed tares among the wheat, and went his way. But when the blade was sprung up, and brought forth fruit, then appeared the tares also. So the servants of the householder came and said unto him, Sir, didst not thou sow good seed in thy field? From whence then hath tares? He said unto them, An enemy hath done this. The servants said unto him, wilt thou then that we go and gather them up?…
>
> The field is the world: the good seed are the children of the kingdom; but the tares are the children of the wicked one; the enemy that sowed

them is the devil; the harvest is the end of the world; and the reapers are the angels.

The parable vividly illustrates the addition of falsehood to falsify otherwise credible information. In other instances, however, credible information may be removed to make a nuisance of otherwise useful information. The prophet Joseph Smith's Translation (JST) of the Holy Bible illustrates several examples of deleted information in both the Old Testament and New Testament. An example is illustrated in Hebrews 7:1–3. The first two verses are the same in the original translation and the JST. The third verse is, however, very different.

> For this Melchizedek, King of Salem, Priest of the Most High God, who met Abraham returning from the slaughter of the Kings, and blessed him: To whom Abraham gave a tenth part of all; first being interpreted King of Righteousness; and after that also King of Salem, which is King of Peace. (Hebrews 7:1–2)

> Without father, without mother, without descent, having neither beginning of days, nor end of life; but made like unto the Son of God; abideth a priest continually. (Hebrews 7:3)

> For this Melchizedek was ordained a priest after the order of the Son of God, which order was without father, without mother, without descent, having neither beginning of days, nor the end of life. And all those who are ordained unto this priesthood are made like unto the Son of God, abiding a Priest continually. (Hebrews 7:3 JST)

Similarly, in Genesis 14:25–40, which gives a detailed

account of the great Melchizedek, have been deleted completely. (See appendix 9.)

The Latter Day Scriptures are not spared this meddling by the adversary, as we read in Moses 5:12–13: "And Adam and Eve blessed the name of God, and they made all things known unto their sons and their daughters. And Satan came among them, saying; I am also a son of God; and he commanded them, saying: Believe it not; and they believed it not, and they loved Satan more than God. And men began from that time forth to be carnal, sensual and devilish." In this example, Satan has actually removed facts fed to Adam's children making them not to believe in their parents.

A few other examples need to be taken notice of. Apart from sowing tares and deleting valuable information from the written word, the devil has yet other weapons. Satan uses deceit and false representation as in that cases of the voice of the devil being used by the mouth of the snake to deceive Eve, and the voice of the devil being used by the mouth of Eve to convince Adam.

Now Satan desires to convince all of mankind. Two men go to a Christian church to marry as husband and wife. Man has been convinced, and even priests, that there was nothing wrong with Sodom and Gomorrah. He still uses Eve's mouth to influence us, as recorded in Moses 5:11: "And Eve, his (Adam's) wife, heard all these things and was glad, saying: Were it not for our transgression we never should have had seed, and never should have known good and evil, and the joy of our redemption, and the eternal life which God giveth to all the obedient." Again we see his influence in 2 Nephi 2:22–23: "And now, behold, if Adam had not transgressed he would not have fallen, but he would have remained in the garden of Eden. And all things which were created must have remained in the same state in which they were after they were created: and they must have remained forever; and had no end. And they would have had no children; wherefore they would have remained in a state of innocence, having no joy, for they knew no misery; doing no good, for they knew no sin." Additionally, 2 Nephi 2:25 states that "Adam fell that man must be; and men are that they might have joy."

The foregoing quotations have an admixture of falsehood and truth. We must therefore be wise and not swallow hook, line, and sinker, as it were. When statements come from apparently respectable mouths with incongruous and diametrically opposing teachings, then we must suspect an enemy who forces to push his own agenda like the tares that the Master Teacher has illustrated so vividly in his parable. The unsuspecting disciple is easily tricked to swallow hook, line, and sinker. We must pray for guidance and teaching by the Master Teacher to identify deceit and avoid it.

Following are some questionable observations.

- The devil speaks by the mouth of the snake (Genesis 3).
- The devil works through Peter to influence the Lord to avoid the atoning sacrifice (Matthew 16).
- The devil teaches Korihor to teach contrary to what he knew to be true (Alma).
- The devil speaks by the mouth of Eve that she never would have had seed if they had not disobeyed God (Moses 5:11).
- The devil teaches that if Adam had not fallen, then all of God's creation would have remained forever as they were made and there would have been no change (2 Nephi 2:22–23).

- Satan dissuades the children of Adam not to believe what they had been taught by their parents about God (Moses 5:12–13).

With technological advancement, we must know that Satan is not excluded; he will use modern, sophisticated technological inputs to be equal with our time. This is already on TV screens at home. We must be warned.

If the transgression in the garden of Eden was not an offence, then listen to what happened thereafter. "Unto the woman God said, I will greatly multiply thy sorrow and thy conception; in sorrow thou shalt bring forth children…" (Genesis 3:16). Is this the best that Eve wanted for her daughters?

Satan, the villain, uses every available type of knowledge, such as the voice of the Lord by the mouths of angels. (See Alma 13:22).

Satan uses the mouths of trusted, respectable people to mouth his voice, to make his voice appear authentic and thus acceptable. The apparent source of a voice is not always genuine and can be faked. So be as wise as the snake, and watch out for surprises.

We never should have had seed if we had continued to obey God. **(See Genesis 1:28.)** If we had continued to obey God, we never would have known the eternal life which God gives unto all the obedient. (See Genesis 3:13.)

We should debate Eve's pronouncements regarding whether they make sense or whether the devil, as usual, used her to mouth the voice of the devil himself.

To conclude our investigations of the ways and ambitions of Satan, we must know that he has impersonated God the Father himself on a number of occasions. Chapter 1 of the Book of Moses in the Pearl of Great Price is a must-read for all. It shows

Satan's persistent efforts to impersonate God the Father. He was found out by Moses and defeated.

Moses was born 1571 BC. The Exodus of Israel from Egypt started in 1491 BC, when Moses was eighty years old. These dates are according to records available in a Bible dictionary. These dates mean that Moses was alive 1,571 years before Jesus Christ. At the beginning of his ministry, Jesus was about thirty years old. Satan tried to deceive him, pretending that he was God the Father. That was after the forty days of fasting day and night, when he must have been very hungry, tired, and weak. After rigorous efforts to overcome Jesus Christ at the end of the days of fasting, Jesus simply dismissed Satan. (See Matthew 4:2.)

From that time, Jesus began to preach and to say, "Repent; for the kingdom of God is at hand." We must be strong in our relationship with and faith in Jesus Christ in order to be able to identify that villain Satan when he plays his tricks, seeking to ditch us. When we attain this relationship with Jesus Christ and God the Father, it will help us to identify Satan and defeat him.

APPENDIX 11

JEBUS

Although Sodom and Gomorrah were destroyed because of sodomy, some Israelite communities had also become interested in this abominable lifestyle. This is illustrated by the sordid story of the Sodom-like behaviour of Benjamites told in the Book of Judges, chapters 19 and 20.

A Levite and his concubine were travelling late in the day with his male servant on their asses. The father of the lady had delayed their departure for five days, and he still wanted them to spend another night.

> But the man would not tarry that night, but he rose up and departed, and came over against Jebus, which is Jerusalem; And when they were by Jebus, the day was far spent: and the servant said unto his master, come, I pray thee, and let us turn into this city of the Jebusites, and lounge in it. And his master said unto him, we will not turn aside into the city of a stranger, that is not of the children of Israel; we will pass over to Gibea. (Judges 19:10–12)

The full story is worth reading, but that is not necessary for the subject of Jebus. Jebus was a hill fortress which maintained its independence until stormed by David as narrated in 2

Samuel 5:7–9: "Nevertheless David took the stronghold of Zion: the same is the city of David. And David said on that day, whosoever getteth up to the gutter, and smitest the Jebusite, and the lame and the blind, that are hated of David's soul; he shall be chief and captain… So David dwelled in the fort, and called it the city of David."

This evidence will put to rest many of the arguments and the numerous questions as to who the original owners of Jerusalem were. Jerusalem was built by the Canaanite Jebusites, and David took it by might.

APPENDIX 12

DISEMBODIMENT

T he living person, otherwise known to be a living soul, has three components. Elements of the earth, also called dust or soil, are brought together in suitable proportions and moulded into the body, or form, of the person as a three-dimensional work of art.

The spirit man existing in heaven was brought down, fused, and kneaded with the earthen body inseparably into the soul of the man, which is lifeless. God then breathed into the lifeless soul of the man, and the man became a living soul.

The lifeless statue form of the man has no motion; the spirit, however, did move on his own before he was compounded into the soul of the man, which is lifeless and not mobile but has supple skin. The living soul is thus a triple combination of the earthen statue of human form, the spirit man from heaven who now possesses the body, and the enabling third component, the breath of life from God, the creator of all.

Disembodiment simply refers to taking back the body that was given to the spirit man from heaven. When this is done, the breath of life goes back to whoever gave it. Now that the spirit is dispossessed of the other two components, he flies away. The spirit is only an existing being and not a living being. This spirit that had a body for life here on earth has now lost the body and now is a disembodied spirit. This is what comes to mind when one talks about a ghost.

By tradition, a ghost is a spirit that once enjoyed the possession of a body that has now been taken away from him. This is the result of Grandpa Adam's disrespect for the law that God gave to him in the garden of Eden. The body will be given back to him again in the process known as the resurrection. He will then come to live again as he was before his first mortal death. This resurrected soul of a man, living for a second time, is immortal and will not die again as he did before. He is back to the status of Adam before God pronounced on him, "Dust thou art and unto dust shall thou return." Now the sin of Adam that brought death to man has been fully erased by the atonement of Jesus Christ. Now the man is responsible for his own activities while he lived on Earth. In this state of our resurrected soul, he will be brought to the court of God to answer questions of his thought, his words that he spoke, and all of his actions while he lived as a mortal man.

Jesus Christ offered himself voluntarily in the process of the atonement as a propitiation to invalidate the curse that Adam brought upon all of us; it is he that will sit in the judgement seat. He will ask questions to probe your life's activities from birth to death. He is meekly and attentively seeking to satisfy himself that apart from doing forbidden things, you indeed sincerely repented from every wrongdoing before your mortal death. And what are some examples of forbidden things? One is murder; another is sin against the Holy Ghost.

The one third of the spirits who joined Satan to rebel against God in heaven are forbidden to enjoy life on earth as humans. Anyone who invokes any of these spirits and thus becomes a medium himself or makes it possible for idols to become mediums for these spirits to speak or act as human beings is allowing them to perform forbidden acts. This is evidently the sin of witchcraft.

APPENDIX 13

THE ONLY LIVING AND TRUE GOD

"By these things we know that there is a God in heaven, who is infinite and eternal, from everlasting to everlasting the same unchangeable God, the framer of heaven and earth, and all things which are in them; And that He created man, male and female, after his own image and his own likeness, created he them; And gave unto them commandments that they should love and serve him, the only Living and True God, and that he should be the only being whom they should worship" (Doctrine and Covenants 20:17–19).

There are twenty-four instances of scriptures that refer to the living God. Twelve of these are from the Old and New Testaments combined. The remaining twelve were taken from the Book of Mormon and the Doctrine and Covenants of the Church of Jesus Christ of Latter-day Saints. It is of great value to note also that the quotation above throws more light on the singular and distinctive nature of the only Living and True God. No other scripture points to this truth about the Christian God—that he is the only Living and True God.

Additionally, two scriptures in the New Testament (John 17:3 and 1 Thessalonians 1:9) and three scriptures in the Book of Mormon (Alma 5:13, Alma 7:6, and Mormon 9:26) also add the attribute "true", thus making him the living and true God. "And this is life eternal, that they might know thee the only true God, and Jesus Christ whom thou hast sent" (John 17:3). These attributes of the only living and true God indicate that there are other gods in addition to this distinct one who are not living. "Though there be many that are called god."1 **Corinthians 8:5**

This article seeks to establish the distinction between the Only Living God and the several other gods. It is necessary to examine the etymology and meaning of the word "god" and also whatever attributes there are which pertain to a god.

According to the compact edition of the *Oxford English Dictionary*, there are two Aryan roots of the original word: "1. to invoke, 2. to pour or offer sacrifice". The original word has thus come to be variously interpreted as "what is to be invoked" or "much invoked", and also "what is worshipped by sacrifice" or "an object of worship." All of these interpretations are plausible. Some scholars accept another meaning of the root which means "to pour" and thus emphasizes the importance of a molten image. The most likely school of thought, however, should have been "worship by pouring libation", as is done by some heathen religions. But lest we forget, let us have a quick look from another angle.

On his first arrival at Luz, between Benjamin and Ephraim in the land of Canaan, Abraham built an altar to honour God. Two generations later, Jacob was at the same place, and he had a dream in the night.

> And Jacob awaked out of his sleep, and he said, surely the LORD is in this place; and I knew it not. And he was afraid, and said, How dreadful is this place! This is none other but the house of God, and this is the gate of heaven. And Jacob rose up early

in the morning, and took the stone that he had put for his pillows, and set it up for a pillar, and poured oil on top of it. And he called the name of that place Beth-el; but the name of that city was called Luz at the first [a Canaanite name]. (Genesis 28:16–19).

This was before Jacob and his family went to Egypt. On his way with his wives and family and all his property, he came to Luz (Beth-el.) And he built there an altar, and he called the place El-beth-el, because there God appeared to him when he fled from the face of his brother. (See Genesis 35:7.) God visited him again in Canaan, following which Jacob (now Israel) set up a pillar of stones, and he poured a drink offering thereon, and he poured oil thereon. And Jacob called this new place Beth-el (in Canaan).

It is now evident that in the pre-Christian era, even in Israel, the way of worship was basically the same across the board. Bulls, lambs, goats, etc. were used for peace, sin, etc. In the original pre-Christian sense, the word "god" referred to a superhuman masculine person worshipped as having power over nature and the fortunes of all mankind.

When the word is applied to the One Supreme Being, this sense is more or less modified, and demons, as supernatural powers of inferior rank, are distinguished from the gods of Greek mythology. When the one True and Living God was accepted and established in the cities, the false gods of mythology continued to be worshipped in the countryside, in the heaths, and were referred to as heathen gods.

Baal, which means "Lord" and also "Possessor", was the sun god and the male, or generative, principle in nature. He was worshipped in different places with different ideas and rites and, of course, different names. Baal was called the following various names in the following places:

- Baal-peor by Moabites and others
- Baal-berith at Sechem
- Baal-Zebub at Ekron (far west of Jerusalem)
- Bel in Babylon
- Zeus in Greece

A distinction was made between God the maker, the being who made the heavens, the earth, and its people and who is believed to have an effect on all things; and god, a spirit or a being believed to control some part of the universe of life and often worshipped for doing so, or a representation of the being, which may be a stone, a tree, a river, a mountain, or even the sun or some other object.

SOME ATTRIBUTES OF A GOD

The living are people who are still alive and therefore are fully constituted with "whole spirits and soul and body", as Paul describes in 1 Thessalonians 5:23. (See Genesis 2:7 and Doctrine and Covenants 88:15, the latter of which says "And the spirit and the body are the soul of man.") This is in contrast to a being, which is a person or a thing that exists. Beings are things in a state of existing that are not necessarily alive.

SPIRITS

By some, "spirit" is explained as a supernatural, incorporeal, rational being or personality regarded as imperceptible at ordinary times to human senses. However, it is capable of being visible at its pleasure and is frequently conceived of as troublesome, terrifying, or hostile to mankind. It is also the form of a dead person, similar to a ghost, or the presence of a dead person which one cannot feel but can see, it being translucent.

To others, "spirit" is the conscious intelligent individual entity that had an existence previous to mortality. All spirit is matter but is more refined and pure than mortal elements.

MAN

In the process of creating man, God said, "Let us make man in our image, after our likeness" (Genesis 1:26; 2:17). "So the gods went down to organize man in their own image, in the image of the Gods to form they him, male and female to form they them" (Abraham 4:27).

"And the Gods formed man from the dust of the ground and took his spirit (that is the man's spirit) and put it into him; and breathed into his nostrils the breath of life, and the man became a living soul" (Abraham 5:7). Thus every living soul is made up of a body and a spirit in union, and they separate into a dead body and a spirit being which cannot be said to be alive. Spirits are never said to be living beings.

In the process of the resurrection, however, the spirit and the body shall be reunited in perfect form. Thus the mortal body is raised into an immortal body—that is, from the first death into life—that it can die no more. The spirits unite with bodies, never to be divided; thus the whole becomes spiritual and immortal, and they can no longer see corruption. (See Alma 11:43–45).

The Resurrected Jesus Christ

"Behold my hands and my feet, that it is I myself: handle me and see; for a spirit hath not flesh and bones, as ye see me have" (Luke 24:39). During his mortal existence, the lord Jesus Christ had occasion to comment on the Father being alive.

God Is alive

"For as the Father hath life in himself; so hath he given to the Son to have life in himself. And hath given him authority to execute judgement also, because he is the Son of Man... As the Living Father hath sent me, and I live in the Father: so he that eateth me, even he shall live by me" (John 5:26–27; 6:57).

The above statements by Jesus Christ himself must be known to all Christians, for every one of them must have referred to their "Living God" at one time or the other. And if God is a living being, the man whose son is Jesus Christ, the Son of Man, then what is the nature of God, the God of the Christians? But first let us look at the other gods—the non-living gods, as opposed to the only living and true God of the Christians.

Non-Living Gods

When the Athenians took Paul to Areopagus and demanded to know the new doctrine that he was declaring to the people, he said to them "...as I passed by, and beheld your devotions (ie sacred, venerated objects), I found an altar with this inscription, TO THE UNKNOWN GOD" (Acts 17:21–23). Before the children of Israel crossed the Jordan river into the Promised

Land, Moses reminded them that they have covenanted with the Lord their God not to make a graven image, or the likeness of anything which the Lord God has forbidden. Otherwise they would be scattered among the nations where they would serve gods, the work of man's hands, wood and stone, which neither see, nor hear, nor eat, nor smell. (See Deuteronomy 4:23–28).

When Belshazzar lifted himself against the Lord of heaven and drank wine from the vessels taken from the house of the Lord; praising the gods of silver and gold, or brass, iron, wood, and stones, which see not, nor hear, nor know, he was destroyed by writing on the wall that read "MENE, MENE, TEKEL, UPHARSIN" (See Daniel 5:22–28).

Abraham's account of his life in Chaldea talks about offering men, women, and children unto strange gods. "These virgins were offered up because of their virtue; they would not bow down to worship gods of wood and stone, therefore they were killed upon this altar, and it was done after the manner of the Egyptians" (Abraham 1:12).

Nature worship in one form or another as appears in the references above and many more is idolatry. Idols represent the various kinds of objects of worship among heathen nations. The Egyptians worshipped the sun and other heavenly bodies, the Nile, and sacred animals, especially the bull. Ra was the sun god, the active power in creation and the giver of life. In Canaan and western Syria, Baal was the sun god a source of life, and Ashtoreth was the corresponding female deity. Each nation had its own peculiar god to whom it ascribed its prosperity and misfortunes. Idolatrous Israel either made images that stood for Jehovah or worshipped one of the gods of the heathen nations around them.

The priests of these idol worshippers invoked spirits to enter and possess the idols. They often possessed the priest himself, whereupon, using the priest as a medium, the spirit was able to do forbidden things and talk as a living human being. This is a rebellion against the command of God. After Samuel had rebuked Saul for an unauthorized sacrifice, he remarked, "... for rebellion is as the sin of witchcraft, and stubbornness is as iniquity and idolatry" (1 Samuel 15:22–23).

One might ask, which are these spirits that would defy God and operate through mediums of idols, humans, etc.? Of course, Satan was the first to demonstrate the practice when he spoke via the mouth of the serpent. (See Moses 4:7). In the country of the Gadarenes, a man with an unclean spirit proclaimed that Jesus was the son of the Most High God and said, "My name is legion, for we are many, and all the devils besought him saying, send us into the swine, that we may enter into them" (Mark 5:1–13; Luke 8:30, 33).

These spirits, devils which are seeking to be housed in any object, living or inanimate, human or whatsoever, will readily respond to invocation by people. And they will be worshipped as gods. The origins of these evil spirits, devils, is not farfetched.

The Book of Revelation says that there was war in heaven and the rebels against God did not prevail; neither was their place found any more in heaven. This group was made up of their leader, Satan, the devil, and his angels, and they were cast out to the earth. And his tail drew the third part of the stars of heaven and cast them to the earth. (See Revelation 12:4, 7–9).

These rebellious spirits were banned from participating in God's plan to send his obedient spirit children to the earth with bodies of flesh and bones. It is illegal for a rebellious spirit to possess bodies, and anyone who allows them access to his or her body is as rebellious as the devils. And rebellion is akin to the sin of witchcraft. (See 1 Samuel 15:23). They are witches. (See Hebrews 12:9).

Thus the devil and his angels are denied the experience of

mortal bodies and earthly life. Without bodies, spirits cannot have the fullness of joy. (See Doctrine and Covenants 93:33–34). And yet equally rebellious people, witches, invoke them, making themselves mediums, via which these rebellious spirits, demons, avail themselves of that which God has forbidden them (for they are encouraged to perform forbidden things).

These gods include the rebellious spirits who are invoked by idol worshippers of heathen gods, whose spirits animate those objects made by the hands of man. (See Jeremiah 2:11). These people become priests to these spirits which are called gods—heathen gods. Though these are called gods, whether in heaven or in earth (as there are many gods and lords), for us there is but one God, the Father, of whom are all things, and we in him and our Lord Jesus Christ, by whom are all things, and we are by him. (See 1 Corinthians 8:5–6).

Is Man a God?

The devil would certainly not be taken seriously when he said, "For God knows that in the day ye eat thereof, then your eyes shall be opened, and ye shall be as gods, knowing good and evil (Genesis 3:5). But not when the Lord God said, "Behold, the man has become as one of us to know good and evil" (Genesis 3:22). There are several other quotations that illustrate that man has potential of a god.

The Jews wanted to stone Jesus "because that thou, being a man, makest thyself God." Jesus answered them, "Is it not written in your law, I said, ye are gods?" (John 10:33–34, Psalm 82:6) and all of you children of the most high. Wherefore, as it is written, they are gods, even the sons of God (D&C 76:58). Because we are the offspring of God (Acts 17:29), we are heirs with Christ (Romans 8:17). Then shall they be gods, because they have no end… because they have all power, and the angels are subjects unto them (D&C 132:20).

JESUS CHRIST

As to the nature of Jesus Christ there must be no argument. For while he was born and lived a mortal life with spirit, body and breath of life: in his temporal death his spirit was disembodied for a short period of three days. But on the third day his spirit was reunited in the process of the resurrection of the dead, and he came back to life again being reconstituted as spirit and body in permanent reunion. With this refined and resurrected body the Lord appeared to his disciples in a locked room where he said, "For a spirit hath not flesh and bones as ye see me have" (Luke 24:29), and in this same form he was seen in vision by Stephen, "The Son of Man standing on the right hand of God" **(Acts 7:56)**. Evidently, Stephen must have seen two personages, one of whom he knew as the Lord Jesus Christ and the other he must have been inspired to know as God the Father. There are several scriptures that support what Stephen saw in this vision. The first person to have seen God as a living man, like unto himself, was Adam. And in the language of Adam, Man of holiness is his name, and the other name of his Only Begotten is the Son of Man, even Jesus Christ, a righteous judge (Moses 6:57, Exodus 33:11). "And He spake unto Moses face to face as a man speakest unto his friend."

Numbers 12:5–8. And the LORD came down in the pillar of the cloud, and stood in the door of the tabernacle, and called Aaron and Miriam: and they both came forth. And he said, Hear now my words: if there be a prophet among you, I the LORD will make myself known unto him in a vision, and will speak unto him in a dream. My servant Moses is not so, who is faithful in all mine house. With him will I speak mouth to mouth, even apparently, and not in dark speeches; and the similitude of the LORD shall he behold; wherefore then were ye not afraid to speak against my servant Moses? These are to illustrate that there is a similitude of man and his maker.

In the presence of the fall Adam confessed and said, "I heard thy voice in the garden and I was afraid, because I was naked; and I hid myself." From that moment Adam lost the privilege of his spirit's input and of seeing God. Genesis 3:10. Enoch walked with God and he was translated that he should not see death because he pleased God. A detailed account of Enoch is found in the Book of Moses in the Pearl of Great Price chapters 6 and 7.

GOD

The scriptures are replete with instances of righteous men seeing God. Three years previous to Adam's death, he called a meeting of the righteous of his posterity in the Valley of **Adam-ondi-Ahman**. And the Lord appeared unto them, and they rose up and blessed Adam and called him Michael, the prince, the archangel. (See Doctrine and Covenants 107:53–54). God himself invited Moses, Aaron, Nadab, and Abihu, and seventy of the elders of Israel. "And they saw the God of Israel..." (Exodus 24:11). Also they saw God, and they did eat and drink.

In the tabernacle, "the LORD spake to Moses face to face, as a man speakest unto his friend" (Exodus 33:11). But when Moses requested and said, "I beseech thee, show me thy glory" (Exodus 33:18), the Lord said, "...and I will take away mine hand and thou shall see my back parts: but my face shall not be seen" (Exodus 33:23).

APPENDIX 14

THE END OF MAN

Power emanating from the atoning sacrifice of Jesus Christ broke the bonds of physical death. The sacrifice overcame the power of death. This ushered in the resurrection of all. Adam's sin was forgiven. The power of the atonement is for the resurrection only, and it restores all men again to the presence of God.

The atoning sacrifice of Jesus Christ was an extra assignment. The original assignment was to teach man how to return to God. God had said, "We will prove them herewith to see if they would do all things which the Lord their God commanded them." Jesus Christ was chosen as the master teacher, the ambassador of God, to teach man on the earth. Jesus Christ was to teach man to qualify himself to obey God's command.

But when the atonement became necessary, Jesus offered himself. This was in addition to his role as a master teacher. The atonement, as we have learned, became necessary when Adam and Eve, already on the earth as living souls, disobeyed God.

After the resurrection, man continues his journey to immortality and eternal life. At the end of the journey, he will be judged. After judgement he will be assigned to one of the kingdoms. This is where he will live in immortality. Adam's sin plays no part in this judgement. It will depend only on what the individual thought, said, and performed.

Comments/Notes:

Comments/Notes:

Comments/Notes:

Comments/Notes:

Comments/Notes:

Comments/Notes:

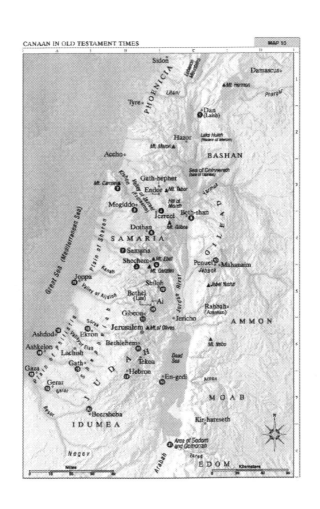

Israel's Exodus from Egypt and Entry into Canaan

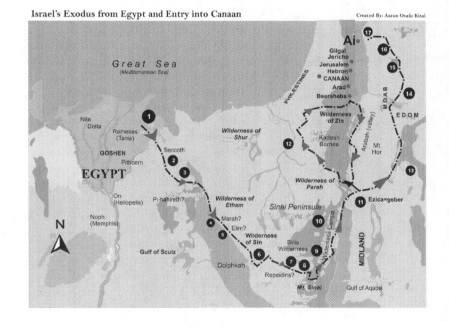

Physical Map of The Holy Land

Created by: Aaron Osafo Kissi

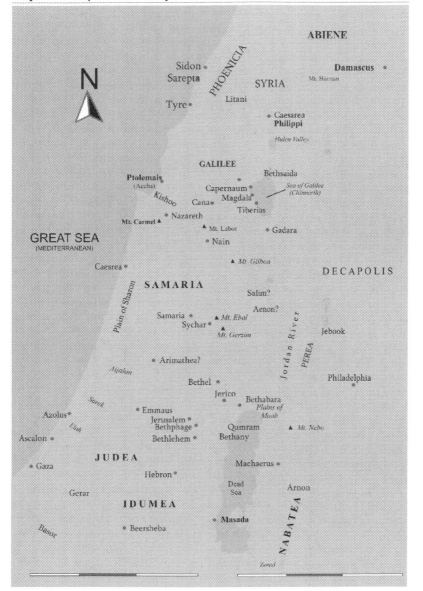

INDEX

Printed in the United States
By Bookmasters